WHAT AFTER 10+2?

By the same author

WHAT THEY DON'T TEACH AT SCHOOL

WHAT AFTER 10+2?

Unconventional career options after school

Vijaya Khandurie

BLUEJAY

Bluejay Books Pvt. Ltd.
A-8/76, Ist Floor
Sector 16, Rohini
Delhi – 110 089
info@bluejaybooksindia.com

First published in 2014 by
Bluejay Books Pvt. Ltd.

10 9 8 7 6 5

Typeset by Eshu Graphic

Printed and bound in India

To all those studying in secondary classes,
and wishing them a bright and successful career.

Contents

Acknowledgements

Though most of the script of this book is written out of the forty odd years of experience I have gathered in the field of school education, yet I made full use of the Internet for the latest in the field of careers. While attending numerous Career Fairs being organised in Delhi from time to time, I was much benefitted to know the latest approach and trends being taken up by various educational as well as professional institutes. Besides these, I am grateful to a few books in the market that deal with subject-specific course studies.

Preface

Students all over the country are very conscious about their careers nowadays. Many professional educational agencies prepare students for entrance examinations conducted throughout the country for various professional courses. Modern-day parents are ready to spend any amount of money on their ward to help them choose a career of their choice.

In competitive times such as these, vacancies in every field of career are limited. Students appearing for these competitions are innumerable. Apart from stiff competitions, huge amount of money seems to be an important factor, particularly in the aviation, engineering and medicinal field.

Courtesy economic growth in India, there is no dearth of options for students after finishing their 10 + 2 or equivalent. Whether a student is brilliant in studies or just mediocre, he/ she can choose out of a lot of fields to choose from to get him into a profitable career. An added advantage in these competitive times is the enthusiasm and talent in the new generation, as also the knack of looking for unconventional courses.

This handy book is especially written for students who are studying in higher secondary schools. It is a sort of guide to help them in choosing their careers. A list of institutions, job profiles and future prospects follow after each career.

Note: The book does not in any way claim to be a definitive guide on all career prospects available to students, but tries to sum up the most opted for options in brief. The institutions suggested for taking up a particular field of study are only the top well-known institutes and the rank can vary with time, place and interest.

We wish you luck in choosing the right career!

1

Career Planning

There was a time when choosing a career meant picking up one of the commonly known professions – engineering, medical, armed forces, teaching, civil services, research, business sector, etc. These jobs required academic excellence and the bright students got selected in competitive examinations after class XII or graduation. The rest went for further studies, or tried their hand at business or other jobs.

But now, the times have changed. With the advent of computers and communication technologies, the scenario has changed completely. There are ample opportunities in practically all the fields, be it banking, hotel management, writing, fashion designing, singing, dancing, playing, et al. Parents today are educated and want their children to get the best possible education. This is one reason why there is massive rush for nursery admissions in reputed schools. Even the uneducated or less educated parents are willing to stretch their limit to get their ward admitted in the so-called 'English medium schools'.

Not just parents, even children these days are more aware of newer opportunities and are willing to try their hand at unconventional career options. Children are not only bright and fast, thanks to parental support and quality education imparted in schools, but also more aware. Up to class VIII, the child is too young to understand or decide what he or she has to become later in life. Class IX onwards the child is mature enough and knows the 'meaning' of 'career'. Earlier, the bifurcation of streams came into effect from class IX – broadly science, humanities and commerce. But now up to Class X, all the subjects are compulsory for students and it is only after clearing class X, that this bifurcation in streams is introduced to make the curriculum more career specific. Nowadays, it is broadly classified as – PCM/PCB, commerce and humanities. When students reach this stage of choosing, they have more or less made up their mind regarding choice of career. Various competitions are held for children after class XII. Those who do not excel in academics have a number of vocational courses to choose from.

If you are interested in a particular field, you have to make up your mind about pursuing it right from class IX. Scoring high marks in the tenth standard enables you to get preference in choosing your desired streams at the higher education level. There is cut-throat competition in all fields of work nowadays. Despite there being an abundance of careers to choose from, the stereotypical choice of high-ranking students is either engineering or the medical profession, followed by MBA and post-graduation, respectively. Besides these, humanities students try their luck with Civil Services of India. Those who are keen to do research, opt for Master's or even a Ph.D. degree.

Divisions of employment

Broadly speaking, we can divide the various academic and professional courses into the following branches:

- Humanities
- Commerce
- Agriculture
- Engineering
- Medical
- Computer science
- Professional courses
- Defence and Allied Forces
- Vocational studies
- Diploma and certificate courses

Before one starts categorising these courses on the basis of their 'essential' nature, it should be noted that every course has its own importance. The nation requires all sorts of experts, ranging from a nuclear scientist to a plumber. It is like the world around us where all sorts of living beings, i.e. humans, animals, rivers, mountains, micro-organisms, etc., co-exist. A complex machine contains a number of simple machines, each with a unique, essential purpose. The machine will stop working if the simpler parts do not work properly or are amiss. So is the case with various professions.

In the coming chapters, we shall describe the various courses that are taught in colleges. It is up to the inclination and interest of a student to choose the one that fits their interests better.

2
Undergraduate Courses

The various undergraduate courses offered in leading universities across the country can be categorised under the following heads:

(a) Humanities-based courses

Bachelor of Arts (B.A. / B.A. Hons.)

There are a number of courses under the humanities banner, both a Bachelor of Arts degree (wherein the students are taught all major subjects falling under the humanities head), and the same degree with honours (wherein there is focus on a subject of choice). The student can take up post-graduation courses for further specialisation after the Bachelor's degree. Those who have interest in social, economic, and political fields of study, or want a degree in Indian and foreign languages, get a chance to expand their grasp on the subjects of their choices in these courses.

Almost all the courses listed asunder are taught in major colleges and universities across the country. A Bachelor's degree (with or without specialisation) is the basic qualification for those aspiring to join civil services, police forces, paramilitary forces, teaching at secondary school level, law, banking, etc. Those having academic interest and willing to be lecturers in schools and colleges take up further education in the form of a Master's degree and further research.

- B. A. (Foreign Languages)
- B.A. (Apparel Design & Merchandising)
- B.A. (Journalism)
- B.A. (Mass Media & Communication)
- B.A. (Tourism)
- B.A. (Hons) Business Economics (BBE)
- B.A. Hons. (Economics)
- B.A. Hons. (English)
- B.A. Hons. (Sociology)
- B.A. Hons. Applied Psychology
- B.A. Hons. Geography
- B.A. Hons. Hindi
- B.A. Hons. History
- B.A. Hons. Music
- B.A. Hons. Patrakarita Evam Jansanchar (Journalism in Hindi)
- B.A. Hons. Philosophy
- B.A. Hons. Political Science
- B.A. Hons. Psychology
- B.A. Hons. Sanskrit
- B.A. Hons. Social Work
- B.A. Hons. Urdu
- B.A. Indian languages (specialisation in any)
- B.A. (Vocational Studies)

(b) Commerce-based courses

Bachelor of Commerce (B.Com.)

With increasing focus on management studies, finance and growth of economy, commerce has come up as a very popular subject among the students. In the present day, money has become very important. Thus, commerce subjects are much sought after by the students. Even those who become engineers or hold degrees in management now enter the financial sector or banking, insurance, chartered accountancy, etc. There is tremendous scope in commerce and opportunities for employment are great. One can go further for a Master's degree to have more command on the subject. The following courses in commerce are taught in practically all the colleges of major universities across the country:

- B.Com. + Cosmic Certified Accountant
- B.Com. Accounts and Finance
- B.Com. Banking and Insurance
- B.Com. Computers
- B.com. Corporate Secretaryship
- B.Com. Foreign Trade
- B.Com. General
- B.Com. Hons.
- B.Com. Hons. in Commerce, Economics and Financial Accounting
- B.Com. Insurance
- B.Com. Professional
- BBA (Bachelor of Business Administration)
- BBE (Bachelor of Business Economics)
- BBS (Bachelor of Business Studies)
- Chartered Accountancy

(c) Science-based courses

Bachelor of Science (B.Sc./ B.Sc. Hons.)

There are hundreds of opportunities in institutions providing studies in science subjects all over India and are ever increasing. One can also continue studying beyond the Bachelor's degree and go ahead with further studies, thereby increasing chances for employment. After graduating in science, one gets opportunities in appearing for various UPSC examinations like Indian Civil Services or Indian Police Services. Those who miss the defence service entrance exams like NDA (which can be taken directly after XII) also get an opportunity to be inducted into the Army, Navy or Air Force. Below is a list of various undergraduate courses in the science subjects:

- B.Sc. Applied Physical Science
- B.Sc. Biochemistry
- B.Sc. Biotechnology
- B.Sc. Business Computing and Information Systems
- B.Sc. Computer Science
- B.Sc. Electronics
- B.Sc. Fashion Technology
- B.Sc. Forensic Science
- B.Sc. Games & Interactive Media
- B.Sc. Hons. Anthropology
- B.Sc. Hons. Biological Sciences
- B.Sc. Hons. Biomedical Science
- B.Sc. Hons. Botany
- B.Sc. Hons. Chemistry
- B.Sc. Hons. Food Technology
- B.Sc. Hons. Geology
- B.Sc. Hons. Home Science
- B.Sc. Hons. Instrumentation
- B.Sc. Hons. Mathematics
- B.Sc. Hons. Microbiology
- B.Sc. Hons. Nursing
- B.Sc. Hons. Physics
- B.Sc. Hons. Polymer Science
- B.Sc. Hons. Statistics
- B.Sc. Hons. Zoology
- B.Sc. Hotel Management, Catering Technology and Tourism

- B.Sc. Information Technology
- B.Sc Interior Decoration
- B.Sc. Life Sciences
- B.Sc. Mass Communication, Journalism and Advertising
- B.Sc. Mathematics
- B.Sc. Medical Laboratory Technology
- B.Sc. Medical Technology
- B.Sc. Microbiology
- B.Sc. Multimedia and Animation
- B.Sc. Natural Sciences
- B.Sc. Nutrition and food Technology
- B.Sc. Physical Education and Sports Sciences
- B.Sc. Physical Sciences
- B.Sc. Physiotherapy
- B.Sc. Plant Biology and Plant Biotechnology
- B.Sc. Radiography
- B.Sc. Textile Designing
- B.Sc. Veterinary Science

(d) Engineering-based courses

Bachelor of Engineering (BE)

- BE Aeronautical
- BE Aerospace
- BE Automobile
- BE Biochemical
- BE Biomedical
- BE Chemical
- BE Civil
- BE Computer Science
- BE Electrical and Electronics
- BE Electronics and Telecommunication
- BE Environmental

- BE Fire Technology and Safety
- BE Genetics
- BE Industrial
- BE Marine
- BE Metallurgical
- BE Optical
- BE Petroleum
- BE Software

Bachelor of Technology (B.Tech.)

- B.Tech. Aerospace Engineering
- B.Tech. Agriculture and Food
- B.Tech. Automobile Engineering
- B.Tech. Bioinformatics
- B.Tech. Biotechnology
- B.Tech. Chemical
- B.Tech. Civil
- B.Tech. Computer Science
- B.Tech. Dairy Technology
- B.Tech. Electrical and Electronics
- B.Tech. Electronics and Telecommunications
- B.Tech. Food Technology
- B.Tech. Industrial Biotechnology
- B.Tech. Information Technology
- B.Tech. Marine
- B.Tech. Mechanical
- B.Tech. Metallurgical
- B.Tech. Paint Technology
- B.Tech. Textile Manufactures

Note: The commonly understood difference between B.E. and B. Tech. is that the former lays more emphasis on the theoretical aspect, while the latter on the practical part of the course.

(e) Medical-based courses:

- Bachelor of Ayurveda Medicine and Surgery (BAMS)
- Bachelor of Unani Medicine and Surgery (BUMS)
- Dental Surgeon (BDS/ BMS)
- Forensic Science
- Health Sciences
- Homeopathy
- Medical Laboratory Technician (MLT)
- Nursing
- Nutritionist and Dietician
- Pharmacist
- Physician/ Surgeon (MBBS)
- Physiotherapy
- Sanitary Inspector
- Veterinary Science

(f) Computer-based courses

* Computer Applications (3 years)
* Engineering in Computer Science (4 years)
* Business Administration (3 years)
* Computing in Computer Science (3 years)
* Graphics and Multimedia (3 years)
* Hardware and Networking (3 years)
* Mathematics in Computer Science (3 years)
* Web Application Development (3 years)
* Web Development (3 years)
* Web Designing and Multimedia (3 years)

(g) Agriculture-based courses

- Agriculture
- Aquaculture
- Horticulture

- Agro Industry
- Dairy Technology
- Fishery Science
- Floriculture
- Poultry Farming

(h) Professional Courses (Bachelor's degree; B.A./ B.Sc.)

In the times of rapid climb up the social ladder, very few people wish to go for regular degrees and focus more on career-oriented courses. There are many institutions that provide professional courses, which make the aspirants expert in a particular field. The demand for professional courses is soaring as it paves ways for good employment opportunities. One can also pursue these courses at the post-graduate level. Following is a list of some subjects that one can take up as a specialisation for a Bachelor's degree:

- Management
- Music
- Hotel Management
- Hotel Management and Catering Technology (BHMCT)
- Shipping (BMM)
- Audiology and Speech Language Pathology (BASLP)
- Business Management (BBM)
- Business Studies (BBS)
- Communication Journalism (BCJ/ BJMC)
- Design (B.Des)
- Fashion Technology (BF Tech)
- Financial Investment and Analysis (BFIA)
- Fishery Sciences (BFS)
- General Law (BGL)
- Information Systems Management (BISM)
- Labour Management (BLM)
- Medical Laboratory Technology (BMLT)

- Medical Record Science (BMRSc)
- Medical Technology (BMT)
- Mental Retardation (BMR)
- Naturopathy and Yogic Sciences (BNYSc)
- Occupational Therapy (BOT)
- Optometry and Vision Science (B.Optom)
- Physiotherapy (BPT)
- Public Relations (BPR)
- Siddha Medical Sciences (BSMS)
- Speech Language & Audiology (BSLA)
- Visual Arts
- Computer Application (BCA)
- Behavioral Healthcare Education (BHEd)
- Fine Arts (BFA)
- Journalism and Mass Communication (BJMC)
- Performing Arts (BPA)
- Travel and Tourism Management (BTM)

(i) Other Degrees

- Bachelor in Mass Media
- Bachelor in Library Science (BLSc/ BLib)
- Bachelor of Architecture (B.Arch)
- Bachelor of Business Management (BBM)
- Bachelor of Business Studies (BBS)
- Bachelor of Communication Journalism (BCJ)
- Bachelor of Divinity (B.D)
- Bachelor of Education (B.Ed; can be pursued after graduation)
- Bachelor of Education in Artificial Intelligence (B.Ed. AI)
- Bachelor of Elementary Education (B.El.Ed)
- Bachelor of Hospitality and Tourism Management (BHTM)
- Bachelor of Information Systems Management (BISM)

- Bachelor of Law (LLB; can be pursued after graduation)
- Bachelor of Laws (BL)
- Bachelor of Library and Information Science (BLIS)
- Bachelor of Literature (B.Lit)
- Bachelor of Medical Technology (BMT)
- Bachelor of Pharmacy (B.Pharma)
- Bachelor of Physical Education (BPE)
- Bachelor of Social Work (BSW)
- Bachelor of Socio Legal Sciences (BSL)
- Bachelor of Veterinary Science (BVSc)
- Basic Training Certificate (BTC)
- Undergraduate Basic Training (UGBT)
- Undergraduate Teacher Training (UGTT)
- Undergraduate Training (UGT)

(j) Vocational courses

It is universally acknowledged that no two students can perform with the same academic brilliance. That does not mean that those who fail to get admissions in university colleges due to lesser marks or financial constraints do not have any viable career options. The basic aim of education is getting an employment. There is no use if somebody pursues higher education without an aim. Vocational education is a wide field where practical education is imparted beside theoretical studies. These courses are most suitable for those who are not interested in academic programmes and long years of education. Taking higher degrees does not guarantee higher income or good employment, but an expert in any vocational subject ensures employment; it could also mean better remuneration than those who go for higher studies. The following list as given by the CBSE (Central Board of Secondary Education) gives an idea of how a student can choose a vocational subject of his choice. The term of these courses can vary, but are mostly for two years:

- Accommodation Services
- Accountancy and Auditing
- Accounting for Business
- Air-conditioning and Refrigeration
- Automobile Technology
- Auxiliary Nursing and Midwifery
- Banking
- Business Data Processing
- Classification and Cataloguing
- Clinical Biotechnology
- Dairying
- DTP, CAD and Multimedia
- Electrical Technology
- Electronics Technology
- Fabrication Technology
- Fashion Design and Clothing Construction
- Food Preparation
- Food Service and Management
- Health Care Sciences
- Health Culture and Beauty Culture
- Horticulture
- Hotel Management and Catering Technology
- Introduction to Financial Market
- IT Application
- IT System
- Library Administration and Management
- Life Insurance
- Marketing and Salesmanship
- Medical Laboratory Technology
- Milk and Milk Products
- Office Secretaryship
- Ophthalmic Techniques
- Poultry, Nutrition and Physiology

- Radio Engineering and Audio Systems
- Reference Service
- Stenography and Computer Application
- Television and Video Systems
- Textile Science
- X-ray Technician

(k) Diploma courses

A diploma is a professional course where a student passing twelfth standard can enter, albeit with certain traits like good command over a language, pleasant personality, self-confidence, and will to work hard. It may not be equivalent to a degree, but it opens the door for a number of employments where money is no constraint. Even graduates can opt for diploma courses. In fact, those who want to do something different from stereotypical work profiles may find diploma courses very useful. Following is a list of disciplines that are offered as diploma courses, though this list is not definitive:

- 3D Animation and Visual Effects
- Advertising and Marketing
- Animation Film Making
- Aquaculture
- Broadcast Journalism for Electronic Media
- Civil Engineering (Army only)
- Computer Integrated Manufacturing
- Dairy Technology
- Equity Arbitrage Trading and Operation
- Event Management
- Event Management and Promotion
- Financial Accounting
- Interior Designing
- Medical Laboratory Technology

- Optometry Technology
- Panchayat Level Administration and Development
- Post Production
- Radio Imaging Technology
- Radio Jockeying
- Sound Engineering
- Television and Broadcasting
- VFX and Digital Film Making
- Youth in Development Work

(l) Certificate courses

Short-term certificate courses – usually ranging from three months to one year duration – are somewhat an additional qualification to your already attained academic, vocational or professional qualifications. Merely getting a certain certificate will not give you a proper employment, but it has the potential to add to your set of skills. There is no end to certificate courses, recognized or non-recognized. Some of these are mentioned below. Many of them are conducted by Indira Gandhi National Open University (IGNOU).

- Agriculture Extension in India
- Bee Keeping (CIB)
- Business Skills (CBS)
- Child Counselling
- Computing (CIC)
- Consumer Protection (CCP)
- Craft and Design Pottery (CCDP)
- Disaster Management (CDM)
- Empowering Women through Self Help Groups (CWDL)
- Environmental Studies (CES)
- Foods and Nutrition (CFN)
- Foods Safety (CFS)

- Guidance (CIG)
- HIV and Family Education (CAFE)
- Human Rights (CHR)
- ICT Applications in Library (CICTAL)
- Industrial Accountant
- Insurance
- Laboratory Techniques (CPLT)
- Labour in Development (CLD)
- Mass Media and Mass Communication
- Nutrition and Child Care (CNCC)
- Nutrition in India
- Participatory Forest Management (CPFM)
- Participatory Project Planning (SAVINI)
- Rural Development (CRD)
- Snow Expert
- Sound Engineering
- Teaching of English as a Second Language (CTE)
- Teaching of Primary School Mathematics (CTPM)
- Tourism Studies (CTS)
- Youth Development Work (CCYP)

(l) Polytechnics

There are various polytechnics run by the Government of India or government-aided agencies that provide training for the work of the following: fitter, painter, draughtsman, surveyor, tool and dye-maker, plastic technology professional, DTP operator, welder, carpenter, plumber, electrician, photographer, embroider, needle work specialist, cook, bookbinder, sanitary inspector, refrigeration and air-conditioning machine engineer, baker and confectioner, radio and television mechanic, computer operator and programming assistant, computer hardware and networking, call centre assistant, data entry operator, front office assistant, even management assistant, office machine operator, among others.

The Industrial Training Institutes (ITIs) run by the Government of India are spread across various parts of India. There are several other polytechnics in abundance that offer such courses.

3

Courses for Humanities Studies

(1) Foreign Languages

Earlier, people used to learn foreign languages as a hobby and there were select institutions like Bhartiya Vidya Bhawan and a few embassies where some foreign languages were taught. Universities were offering courses in selected foreign languages, but not many students pursued the courses to make languages their careers.

Now, the situation is different. With globalisation, the demand of foreign languages has increased considerably. A number of multinational companies (MNCs) are emerging which need interpreters and translators. Every embassy requires the services of translators and interpreters. Since India is an emerging economic power, foreign countries are establishing their base in different parts across India. Translators are also appointed by research institutions, publishing houses and industrial houses for their services.

One of the important aspects of the Indian economy is tourism. As compared to yesteryears, more and more foreigners are visiting India. Thus, inevitably, the demand of interpreters and translators is also increasing. Languages have been included as a part of the curriculum in many schools and colleges across India.

Airlines and hospitality industry also employ and give preference to candidates with knowledge of foreign languages.

Various courses in foreign languages include degree courses, diploma courses and certificate courses, but one could face tough competition in acquiring seats for these courses.

It is noteworthy that various countries require English teachers to teach the subject through their own languages. Every year, a number of Delhi University's post-graduates are recruited by institutions from foreign countries for the same purpose. Those who have a flair for languages really enjoy their jobs. Most of the colleges in universities across India offer regular under-graduate courses in languages. Some courses under the University of Delhi are listed as follows:

Eligibility: Passed twelfth standard in any stream with minimum 45% marks.

Undergraduate Courses:

* B.A. Hons. – German (3 years)
* B.A. Hons. – French (3 years)
* B.A. Hons. – Spanish (3 years)

Institutions offering Language Courses:

- University of Delhi
- Jawaharlal Nehru University (JNU)
- Mumbai University

Bachelor of Arts (Hons.) in the following Foreign Languages: 1. Arabic 2. Chinese 3. French 4. German 5. Japanese 6. Korean 7. Persian 8. Russian 9. Spanish.

The School of Foreign Languages (SOFL) of the Indira Gandhi National Open University (IGNOU) offers certificate courses in Arabic, Persian, French, German, Spanish, Russian, and Japanese.

Contact institutes:

1. School of Foreign Languages (SOFL), IGNOU
   e-mail: sofl@ignou.ac.in
2. Department of Germanic and Romance Studies, University of Delhi
   e-mail: head@grs.du.ac.in
3. School of Languages & Culture (SOLC)
   * B. A. (Hons) – English, German, French, Spanish, Chinese, Hindi (3 years)
   * Certificate of Proficiency – English, French, Spanish, German, Chinese (6 months)
   web: www.sharda.ac.in
4. Amity University
   B.A. Hons – German, French, Spanish (3 years)
   web: www.anity.edu

Placement opportunities:

* Language teacher in schools and colleges
* Government and private offices
* Interpreter
* Various posts in embassies
* Guide at tourist places
* Foreign jobs

(2) **Journalism and Mass Communication**

What do you do in the morning each day? Rush for the newspaper or open the net to read the main news of the previous day, I am sure. Somebody has rightly said, "If a dog bites a man, it is not news; but if a man bites a dog, it becomes a story." In order to present a story to readers as news, the writer has to work hard to make mundane everyday facts read interesting. The job of a journalist is not just to collect and disseminate the news, but also to write the same in style. Journalism includes investigating the news, then analysing the same and finally reporting to the masses through newspapers and mass media.

Journalism works at various levels depending upon the mode of communication used, i.e. print, television, audio, other electronic modes, etc. Similarly, a piece of news could be political, educational, social, religious, cultural, etc. Whether it is a sports event or natural disaster, a reporter has to move to the sight to cover the news. The work of a journalist is very hard. Putting their life at risk at times, they travel to far-flung areas, sometimes riot-affected, under the rage of natural calamities, and also during wars. While on work, they have to keep their eyes and ears open to everything that happens around them; there is no time for them to relax. Their job includes working day and night at odd hours to cover the news.

Everyone is fond of watching TV in their leisure time, whether news or any other shows. For the news that is telecast, the term 'mass media' is used because of it being closely entwined with the masses. A career in journalism is prestigious, and if you make the right moves, pays a lot too. The job of a journalist is multifarious. It not only includes collecting the news, but preparing a draft, editing it, and sending it forward. It is then scrutinised by a team of editors and then finally produced through newspaper or mass media.

Eligibility criteria: 10+2 or equivalent (minimum 45 % marks; could vary with universities and institutes)

Selection criteria: Group discussion and interview

Courses (three years):

* Bachelor of Arts in Journalism and Mass Communication (BAJM)

* B. Sc. – Film & TV Production
* B.A. – Journalism
* Diploma Course (usually one year)

Opportunities in Journalism and Mass Media:

- News Reporter
- News Editor
- News Reader
- Cameraman
- Photo Journalist
- Programme Anchor
- Producer
- Director
- Interviewer
- Feature Writer
- Radio Jockey

Professional Institutes:

1. **Indian Institute of Mass Communication** (IIMC)
   (There are branches in New Delhi, Maharashtra, Mizoram, Jammu & Kashmir, Odisha and Kerala.)
   Web: www.iimc.nic.in
2. **University of Technology and Management** (UTM)
   (BBA in Journalism and Mass Communication; MBA in Media Management.
   Web: www.utm.ac.in
3. **Amity University**
   Web: www.amity.edu
4. **Lovely Professional University**
   (Journalism & Film Production)
   Web: www.lpu.in

Other colleges for courses in Journalism and Mass Communication:

- A.J. Kidwai MCRC, Jamia Millia Islamia, Delhi
- Asian College of Journalism, Chennai
- Indian Institute of Journalism and New Media, Bangalore
- International School of Business and Media, Pune
- Manorama School of Communication, Kottayam
- Mudra Institute of Communications, Ahmedabad
- Symbiosis Institute of Mass Communication, Pune
- Xavier Institute of Communication, Mumbai

Placements: Newspapers, magazines, news channels, production houses, publishing houses, news agencies, freelance jobs, among others.

(3) Advertising

Advertising is a means of persuading masses to purchase the commercial products and services through print or visual media. It's almost every day that we read and view advertising messages in newspapers, magazines, radio and television or other media such as mobiles and websites which make great impact on the minds of people. I am sure you can think of innovative commercial advertisements right now that have left a mark in your memory, or even tempted you to try the product, be it for the product or the celebrity endorsing it, or just the advertisement concept. The art of creative messages to sell is so strong, it influences the potential buyers to a great extent. Mark Twain has rightly said, "Many a small thing has been made large by the right kind of advertising."

Advertising is a highly competitive market. Due to economic liberalization in India coupled with the changing social trends, advertising industry has shown speedy growth in the recent time resulting in the emergence of numerous ad agencies. It is a booming business in India with crores of turnover. Obviously the field of advertising and publicity industry has generated many job opportunities for young people. According to a recent survey, lakhs of people are presently working in the advertising and publicity industry and the demand is constantly growing.

A career in advertising is a lucrative job. If you feel that you are creative, imaginative, have a flair for writing, communication skills and the ability to translate ideas into a visual format, the field of advertising is most suitable for you. Advertising agencies prefer highly creative and talented individuals who can think independently. The crux of advertising is effective communication. Working in an advertisement company will give you opportunities for showing your skills and you will be paid handsome pay packets too. There are openings in newspapers, journals, magazines, commercial section of radio or television, market research organizations and so on.

Eligibility criteria: 10+2 in any stream.

Undergraduate courses:

- BFA (Commercial Art / Fine Arts)
- BA (Advertising)
- BA (Advertising and Public Relations)
- Diploma in Advertising & PR
- Post-graduate Diploma in Advertising & PR

Job profile:

- Advertising manager
- Sales manager
- Public relations officer
- Creative director
- Copy writer

- Visualiser
- Animator
- Photographer
- Marketing manager

Professional Institutes:

1. Indian Institute of Mass Communication, New Delhi www.iimc.nic.in
2. Mudra Institute of Communications (MICA), Gujarat Web: www.mica-india.net
3. Narsee Monjee Institute of Management Studies, Maharashtra Web: www.nmims.edu
4. Xavier's Institute of Communication, Maharashtra Web: www.xaviercomm.org
5. Symbiosis Institute of Media and Communication, Maharashtra Web: www.simc.edu

Other Institutes:

- Bharatiya Vidya Bhawan, New Delhi
- Punjabi University, Punjab
- Madras Christian College (MCC), Tamil Nadu
- University of Delhi, Delhi
- Maharshi Dayanand University (MDU), Haryana
- The National Institute of Advertising, New Delhi

Placements: Major media houses and advertising agencies across the world.

(4) Beauty Culture

For centuries, women have been using varieties of natural herbs to enhance their beauty and personality. Primarily, they give importance to those parts of the body that are openly visible; like hair, eyes, eyelashes, eyebrows, face, nails of fingers and toes, etc. They use *haldi* as a face mask, nail paints, *mehendi* for hands and hair, make-up, and ornaments of all kinds so that they look beautiful and attractive. The trend is continued in modern times as well.

The main objective of imparting skills and knowledge to aspirants attending this course is to help them getting employment as beauticians. The added benefit is that along with working with giants in the salon industry, these trainees can also start their own parlours. The number of girls – educated or not much educated – who are attending such courses is increasing day by day. It only goes to show the popularity of this profession. According to FICCI report, beauty and wellness is an 11,000-crore industry and constantly growing at a rate of 30-35% annually. Further, due to new scientific development, professionals in this field are generating revenues in the larger order. There is huge demand of professionals in this field, not only in India but in many developing countries.

The trainees are taught the anatomy and physiology of the human body besides personality grooming. They are given basic skills in hair cutting and styling, removing unwanted hair through various ways, face and scalp massaging, shampooing, colouring of hair, make-up, and several other things related to hair dressing and beauty.

Eligibility criteria: 10+2 or equivalent

Undergraduate Courses: Usually these are short-term courses (6 to 12 months), and duration may vary with institutes.

- Diploma/Advance Diploma: Cosmetology
- Nutrition and Dietetics
- Professional Make-up
- Spa Therapy

- Hair Designing
- Beauty Culture

Job Profile:

- Cosmetologist
- Beauty therapist
- Beauty consultant
- Hair-stylist
- Make-up artist
- Mehendi expert
- Make-up artist
- Spa and aroma therapist
- Nail artist
- Nutritionist and dietician
- Entrepreneur

Professional Institutes:

1. **VLCC Institute of Beauty & Nutrition, Delhi**
   Web: www.vlccinstitute.com
2. **International Women Polytechnic, New Delhi**
   Web: info@iwponline.net
3. **Eves Beauty Parlour and Academy, Delhi**
   Web: www.evesbeauty.com

Placements: Beauty industry, hotels, fashion industry, cosmetic units, academic institutes, television and film industry, own beauty salon.

(5) Travel and Tourism

Look at the top world cities – New York, London, Tokyo, Paris! These famous cities are some of the biggest foreign exchange earning metropolitan cities in the world. Thousands of visitors from across the world visit these beautiful cities every day. This is one of the main reasons behind their financial prosperity.

Famous Indian cities attract vast number of tourists from all the world. Apart from Agra, where most foreigners visit, Udaipur, Jaipur, Srinagar, Delhi, Leh, Ajmer, Hyderabad, Chennai, Kolkata, Mumbai, and many others are the focal points of tourists' itinerary. Tourism has become a major industry.

India is one of the oldest countries in the world, still maintaining its culture and tradition. Tourism industry in India basically provides quality services to tourists who are away from home and expect enjoyable and trouble free trips.

Tourism is a fascinating career, especially for those who possess pleasant personalities and have excellent command over one or more languages. Communication skills are a must. One must have detailed knowledge of the nation and its tourist destinations.

Eligibility criteria: 10+2 or equivalent in any stream

Undergraduate Courses:

- B. A. – Tourism Administration (3 years)
- Diploma in Destination Management
- Diploma in Airlines
- Diploma in Cargo Operations and Management

Job Profiles in:

- Travel agencies
- Tour operators
- Hotel industry
- Road and air transport
- Holiday consultants
- Government tourism departments
- Tourist guides and interpreters
- Work in International Air transport Association (IATA)

- Information assistants

Professional Institutes:

1. **Amity University:**
   Web: www.amity.edu
2. **Kuoni Academy, New Delhi**
   Web: www.kuoniacademy.co.in
   (Raipur, Ahmedabad, Bhopal, Guwahati, Mangalore, Jabalpur)
3. **Creative Academy of Tourism, New Delhi**
   Web: www.thecreativeacademy.in

Other Institutes:

* University of Delhi, Delhi
* Kurukshetra University, Kurukshetra, Haryana
* Agra University, Agra, UP
* Benaras Hindu University, Varanasi, UP
* Bangalore University, Bangalore, Karnataka
* University of Madras, Chennai, Tamil Nandu
* University of Calcutta, Calcutta, West Bengal
* University of Mumbai, Mumbai, Maharashtra
* University of Poona, Pune, Maharashtra
* Skyline Business School, New Delhi

Placements: Tourism boards, tour operators, global distribution system, travel BPO, airlines, cruises, visa services, hotels, business travel, city guilds, etc.

(6) Acting

Acting is a natural talent, but honing the same in a professional institution certainly helps the finer points of acting in films, TV and video shows, etc. In the early years of the India film industry, educational qualifications did not matter much. Talent was the sole measurement. Children as young as five-year-old showed excellent temperament and became very successful. Many professionals in other fields left their job to enter this highly competent area of entertainment.

In order to be a successful actor, one should possess certain qualities: command over language, clarity in expression, good voice, imagination, will to work hard, etc. Experience perfects the skill in individuals, thereby increasing their demand in the industry. At present, people from the film and TV industry organise many talent-hunt programs for the children who not only become national celebrities but are offered further training to become good actors.

Those who have cleared their secondary education and want to choose acting as a career should join a course in dramatics. The National School of Drama, New Delhi is an institution run by famous actors in the field of dramatics. The school offers diploma course in Dramatic Arts, which is recognized by the Government of India. This course is also the stepping stone for higher posts under the Central Government such as Doordarshan, Akashvani, and prestigious teaching assignments in National School of Drama, New Delhi and Film and Television Institute of India (FTII), Pune under the Ministry of Information and Broadcasting.

Acting is not an easy job; a lot of labour and hard work is required. Even if you become a good actor, there is cut-throat competition. But at the end of the day, one earns glamour, name, fame and money.

Eligibility: 10+2

Professional Institutions:

1. **National School of Drama, New Delhi**
   Web: www.nsd.gov.in

2. **Asian Academy of Film & Television, Noida**
   www.aaft.com
3. **Film and Television Institute of India (FTII), Pune, Maharashtra**
   Web: www.ftiindia.com
4. **The Imago School of Acting, New Delhi**
   Web: www.imagoindia.com
5. **Film and Television Institute of Andhra Pradesh**
   Web: www.filmandtelevisioninstituteofandhrapradesh.com
6. **Taneja's Actors Studios, Mumbai, Maharashtra**
   Web: www.roshantaneja.com
7. **Actor Prepares, Mumbai, Maharashtra**
   Web: www.actorprepares.net

Placements: Except trying their luck in talent hunt shows and film industry, actors can also associate with production houses like Balaji Telefilms Ltd, Cinevista, Pritish Nandi Communications, Sahara one Media and Entertainment Ltd, Saregama India Ltd, Shree Ashtavinayak Cine Vision Ltd, Star TV, UTV Software Communication Ltd for roles on television and modelling assignments.

(7) Modelling

National dailies, periodicals, television commercials and various other media showcase a lot of advertisements and there one sees not only the product, but also the models making the product look ever more attractive. For quite some time, the young generation in India is attracted to modelling. The main objective is fame, name and money. Modelling also is gateway to beauty competitions and eventually, the film industry.

It is essential to note here: not everybody can become a model. There are certain criteria that help young aspirants to enter this fascinating world. A good height, perfect body, photogenic face, and charming looks are some of the basic attributes that give advantage in this profession. If you are ready to work hard at odd hours of the day, are self-disciplined, mobile and ready to go anywhere for shooting at any time, modelling will suit you. Clear voice and good facial expressions will be an added advantage.

Modelling can be done part-time or full time but this career is short-lived for most. After 10-15 years, other young faces arrive on the scene and older ones become redundant. In most cases, middle-aged models opt for acting in TV or if they have managed to make good connections and exhibit exceptional talent while they were actively involved with modelling, they get chances in the film industry. Many good models become successful actors with the passage of time. Some open their own agencies to train youngsters desirous of entering the modelling field.

Eligibility: 10+2

Career opportunities: One can model in advertisements, fashion shows, with fashion designers, in TV Commercials, etc.

Professional Institutes:

1. Atul Kaobekar, Negative Space Photographer, Mumbai.
2. Aditi Modelling Service, Bengaluru.
3. Elite School of Modelling, New Delhi.
4. Soft School of Modelling, New Delhi.
5. The Model, New Delhi.

Placement: in advertising, fashion industry, television and films.

(8) Teaching (Primary Level)

Teaching is one of the oldest professions in the world. The process of teaching-learning came into practice right from the early stages of civilization. Every child needs education, whether formal or informal. Even animals train their newly-born young ones to be defensive and ways to adjust with the surroundings or situations.

The job of a teacher is not as easy as many like to believe. He/ she not only gives knowledge, but also ignites the imagination of a child. They instil the values in the mind of the learner and help them in character building and other requisites through explaining, demonstrating, questioning and motivating. Real education is to bring change in the behaviour of a learner. Rabindranath Tagore once said, "The highest education is that which does not merely give us information but makes our life in harmony with all existence." A good teacher can inspire hope and instil a love of learning.

Gone are the days when a person did his M.A. without a goal and after getting no 'proper' job became a teacher. Such notion is no more applicable in modern times. Go to any primary or secondary school, you will find intelligent and smart teachers taking care of students. Teachers play a very important role in society as they build the foundation of the country's future.

The new methods of innovative teaching-learning techniques have replaced the traditional methods of teaching. New teaching aids like computers, virtual learning classrooms, projectors and even simulation aids are very common nowadays.

There are three stages where a teacher is required – primary schools, secondary schools, and in university colleges. Since the present book is meant for students who have completed 10 + 2, we shall focus only on Primary education, i.e. from nursery to class V. However, a teacher can do graduate and post-graduate courses, and further his/ her qualifications by doing research on education to get higher and better jobs.

Teaching nursery and primary classes is the most difficult. A primary school teacher needs to have enthusiasm for the subjects they teach.

In order to become a primary school teacher, one should get through 10 + 2 in any stream of subjects like humanities, commerce, science, etc. Afterwards, they can seek admission for getting Diploma in Nursery Primary Teacher Training (NPTT; usually a two-year-long course), Nursery Teacher Training Programme (NTT; one year course), or enrol in District Institutes of Education and Training (DIET)s which are situated throughout India. The training helps teachers to learn about creative ways of teaching, child development, Montessori education, health and nutrition, computer awareness, etc.

Eligibility: 10+2 (any stream)

Courses:

- 2-year Diploma in Nursery Primary Teacher Training (NPTT)
- 1-year Diploma in Nursery Teacher Training (NTT) Programme
- 2-years Diploma in District Institutes of Education and Training (DIET)

Note: There are many private institutes and polytechnics providing these courses too.

Career Opportunities: Post these courses, candidates can work as nursery teachers, primary teachers, at adult education centres, and can have their own play school or NGOs.

Professional Institutes:

1. District Institute of Education and Training (with centres across the country)
   Web: www.delhi.gov.in/Courses
2. Indira Gandhi Institute of Advance Education, New Delhi
   Web: www.nurseryteachertraining.com

3. International Women Polytechnic, New Delhi
   Web: www.iwponline.net

Placements: Government schools, private schools, establishing own school, NGOs.

(9) Career in Music Industry

For those students who have a natural inclination to music and want to adopt music as a career, there is lot of scope in India as well as abroad. After a degree in music, you can work as an individual or in a group. With the growth of entertainment requirements of the masses, music has become an industry. With experience and practice you can enhance your talent to earn a decent remuneration. The only thing you require is a deep interest in music.

Institutions dealing with music courses: Though almost every school, college and university offers music as a subject, the following colleges are more prestigious and award degree or diploma in music:

1. University of Kolkata, West Bengal
2. Ramjas College, University of Delhi, Delhi
3. Bengaluru University, Karnataka
4. Bharatiya Sangit Mahavidyalaya, Gwalior, Madhya Pradesh
5. Annamalai University, Tamil Nadu

After attaining the degree/diploma, the aspirant can join the following careers:

(a) **Teaching:** Unlike other subjects taught in schools and colleges, teaching music is a viable option. Music is an essential part of various functions that are conducted by every school and college.

A music teacher can also take private tuitions. A clear advantage of it is the flexibility of time between a teacher and a student. Even those who are employed elsewhere and are music enthusiasts look for music teachers to sharpen their music talents. The spread of musical industry can be gauged from the fact that talent contests and various types of musical shows organised by entertainment channels in Indian televisions have become very popular. Talented singers launch their own music albums. There is no dearth of opportunities for good singers and instrumentalists in the field of advertisement and live shows. Moreover, apart from good money, these people get recognition and awards too. Opening a music school is also one way of earning in this field.

(b) **Radio and video jockey**: Hundreds of channels on Indian television and radio require people with melodious voices to entertain the audiences.

(c) **Music production and direction**: Because India has a rich and ancient culture, music paves the way of various genres of music to the budding artists. Whether it is Hindustani classical music, Carnatic music or pop songs, most people like them in their spare times. Those adept in any form of music can get opportunities in radio, television or film industry as producers and directors. It requires professionalism and experience which comes with time.

(d) **Music therapy:** Healing through music is a therapy fast gaining grounds. Human beings respond to different types of sounds in different ways and can be used to provide music therapy to people suffering from loneliness, physical pain, depression, high stress, etc.

Other than the above, experts in music are also required as musicologist, music business attorney, music reporter, Music performers, architectural acoustic consultant, arts administrator, etc.

(10) Photography

Photography is a science as well as an art. In fact, whatever we see on television, films, videos, etc., everything is concerned with photography. Whether it is space travel or deep sea pictures, micro insects or macro galaxies, all these are most clearly witnessed through photographs. There is hardly any field where photography is not involved.

Photographyhasmanydimensions.Aprofessionalphotographer does not need much of formal education. Some want photography as a hobby; others look to earn their living through this medium. Photography as an art requires artistic nature and creative mind. Leading photographers have made portrait photography as their career (note Philippe Halsman, Yusuf Karsh, and Raghu Rai, Ashwin Gatha among many Indian photographers). Now every person, holding a mobile phone with a camera can take instant pictures. Millions of people exchange personal imaging in the cyber space through their mobile phones.

Wedding photography is very common as people wish to capture their special moments forever. This is one of the few occasions when all the relatives and close friends assemble and enjoy the feast. This type of photography is usually done independently or with the help of some staff. There is lot of labour covering all the activities but it fetches good money. A wedding photographer needs sophisticated photo equipment to present good photographs and videos.

Portrait photography is the simplest type. It involves the use of a good camera and lighting. One should have a studio for this purpose. Everybody requires a passport-size photos for numerous purposes. A skilled portrait photographer focuses on the subject's face and the expression on it. While taking a photograph of Einstein, the photographer Phillip Halsman asked the great scientist about the atom bomb just before pressing the button. Within no time the inner feelings generated on his face and Halsman clicked. It became one of the best photographs of Einstein. Group photography, which is also a part of portrait photography, is as popular now as it was before.

Fashion photography is another area which is much in demand. There are fashion shows every now and then. A fashion photographer shoots either in studios or on locations. He/ she also gets a chance to get his photographs published in fashion magazines. Whether the location is on the ramp or outdoor, he gets a chance to show his creativity. He should have a complete knowledge of lighting, colours and a keen eye for aesthetics, artistic flair and ability to take photographs in the available light. There is plenty of money in this business.

Wildlife photography is most suitable for those who have a penchant for adventure and travelling, and love for animals. Besides having a keen eye on animals' behaviour and nature, he must possess technical knowledge. He must have a lot of patience. At times one has to spend many nights to take a single shot, depending on the mood of a particular animal. Before venturing into this field, it is always better to learn the basics from a senior wildlife photographer. Initially there is not much money, but if you have the zeal and patience, you may earn name, fame and money. Remember, "a picture is worth a thousand words".

Eligibility: 10+2 in any stream. Those who have acquired some formal education can also become photographers.

Courses: Some professional institutions give training but otherwise, no formal courses are available for photography. An aspirant can learn under a professional photographer or in a studio.

Types of photography:

- Advertising
- Aerial
- Architectural
- Digital

- Documentary
- Fashion and Glamour
- Forensics
- Industrial
- Landscape
- Mobile phone
- Paparazzi
- Portrait
- Sports
- Still life
- Technical
- Underwater
- Wedding
- Wildlife

Professional Institutions:

1. **National Institute of Photography, Mumbai, Maharashtra**
   Web: www.focusnip.com
2. **Delhi College of Photography, Delhi**
   Web: www.dcop.in
3. **Pearl Academy, Delhi**
   Web: www.pearlacadeny.com
4. **Raghu Rai Center for Photography, Gurgaon, Haryana**
   Web: www.raghuraicenterforphotogrophy.com

Placements: Freelancing, film/TV studios, open own studio, tourist spots, portfolios, for aspiring models and actors, artistic photography, publication houses/ for books, among others.

(11) Fine Arts

As per the definition of fine arts, it is visual art created primarily for aesthetic purposes and valued for its beauty or expressiveness, specifically, painting, sculpture, drawing, graphics, music, dancing, poetry, or architecture. It is any art created for its own sake, as opposed to commercial artwork. According to the theory of fine arts, the smaller the base, the greater is the fine arts. A painter needs paper or canvas, a dancer needs floor, a musician needs some instrument, a sculptor needs clay or stone. All these fine arts need some base. That way, poetry or vocal music is the finest of the fine arts. John Ruskin has aptly summarised, "Fine art is that in which the hand, the head, and the heart of man go together."

The main objective of the fine arts courses is to make students understand the basics of art history, aesthetics and art appreciation. They would be made aware of different types of visual art forms as well as techniques employed therein. It can be learnt through the lectures, reading, gallery visits, visits to the art historical sites and hands-on activities, students will develop an understanding of the elements of art and a basic vocabulary for describing and appreciating visual art forms.

An aspirant who wants to enter this beautiful field will have many choices:

Art and Craft, Visual Art, Performing Art, Indian Theory of Rasa and Bhava, Painting (Murals, Miniatures, Easel Paintings), Sculpture (Relief, Round) and Architecture, etc.

The study of the fine arts prepares students for a variety of careers in and out of the arts. Since this field is different from other professions, it has typical opportunities like designing, teaching, graphics, creative visualizer, in dance schools, freelancing, opening own studio, performing at various places, TV, and films. Whatever be your choice, you have to work very hard; popularity, name, fame and money will be at your doorstep.

Eligibility criteria: 10+2 or equivalent (minimum 50% marks)

Courses offered:

- Bachelor of Fine Arts (BFA) (4 years program)
- B.A. (Fine Arts) (3-years program)

Professional Institutes:

1. Amity University
   Web: www.amity.edu
2. Faculty of Visual Arts, Banaras Hindu University, Varanasi, Uttar Pradesh
   Web: www.bhu.ac.in/visualarts
3. Kalabhawan-Vishva Bharati University, Shantiniketan, West Bengal
   Web: www.visva_bharati.ac.in
4. Delhi College of Arts, Delhi
   Web: delhicollegeofart.com

(12) Performing Arts

People in India are proud of their heritage and rich culture under the patronage of kings and rulers since the 2nd century CE, which is also reflected in temples and palaces across the country. Dances, songs, and folk or classical music are linked to numerous ceremonies like births, weddings, religious processions, harvest seasons, etc. Dholak, tabla, sitar, mridanga, and scores of musical instruments and various dance forms show the rich culture of India.

Natyasastra and *Abhinaya Darpana* are two surviving dance documents, thought to have originated around 2200 BC, includes eight classical dance forms, namely, *bharatanatyam, kathak, kathakali, mohiniattam, kuchipudi, yakshagana, manipuri, odissi* and *sattriya* from different regions of India. In addition to that, there are the folk dances of tribal areas that include *bhangra* of Punjab; *bihu* of Assam; *chhau* of Jharkhand; *birhas* and *charkulas* of Uttar Pradesh; *ghoomar* of Rajasthan; *dandiya* and *garba* of

Gujarat; *yakshagana* of Karnataka and *lavani* of Maharashtra.

In order to serve the cause of the performing and allied arts and to establish a national centre for the preservation and promotion of classical, traditional and contemporary performing and visual arts, Sir Dorabji TataTrust donated forty lakh rupees to National Centre for the Performing Arts (NCPA) in Mumbai in the year 1966. This also is the home of the Symphony Orchestra of India, which was established by NCPA in 2006.

A number of educational institutes and universities in India are offering courses in the field of performing arts at different levels certificate, diploma, undergraduate degree, postgraduate degree, and diploma. The aspirants for performing arts can become singers, music composers, dancers, musicians – vocal or instrument – drama artists and even enter film world. Remuneration in the field of performing arts depends upon the talent of the artist as well as the field he/she chooses.

Eligibility criteria: 10+2 or equivalent (minimum 50% marks)

Courses offered: Bachelor of Music

* Classical Hindustani Vocal (3 years)
* Hindustani Classical Instrumental (3 years)
* B.A. (Performing Arts) (3-year program)
* BPA (Bachelor of Performing Arts)

Professional Institutes:

1. Amity University, Nodia, Uttar Pradesh
   Web: www.amity.edu
2. Lalit Narayan Mithila University, Bihar
3. University of Mysore, Karnataka
4. Dr Babasaheb Ambedkar Marathwada University, Maharashtra
5. Chaudhary Charan Singh University, Uttar Pradesh
6. Sri Padmavathi Mahila Visvavidyalayam, Andhra Pradesh

4

Commerce-based Courses

(1) Chartered Accountancy

Nowadays, accountancy has become a very popular course. A chartered accountant is a professional who completes the final level of the chartered accountancy course conducted by the Institute of Chartered Accountants of India (ICAI) and has become a member of the institute. An aspirant should register with the ICAI to appear for the examination held twice every year – May and November. After finishing a two-year course excluding the training period, he becomes a specialist in accounting, auditing and taxation. As per Company Act, only Chartered Accountants are appointed as auditors of companies in India. A qualified Chartered Accountant can join government service or a private firm, or even work independently. Another popular field of accountancy is cost accounting wherein a qualified accountant can pursue for working out the cost involved in a project and does the forecasting of its benefits.

Eligibility criteria: 10+2 or equivalent in any stream

Courses:

* Chartered Accountancy
* Cost & Management Accountant

Career Prospects:

- Private practice as Cost and Management Accountant
- Tax consultancy
- Project management consultant
- Surveyor and loss assessor under Insurance Act
- Recovery consultant in banking sector
- Business valuation advisor.
- Finance management advisor
- Academics as teacher

Professional Institutes:

1. **The Institute of Chartered Accountants of India, Noida** (with regional offices in Mumbai, Kolkata, Chennai and Kanpur)
   Web: www.icai.org
2. **The Institute of Cost Accountants of India, Kolkata**
   Web: www.icmai.in

(2) **Bachelor of Business Administration (BBA)**

The BBA programme comprises commerce and business administration, general business and advanced courses for specific purposes. The course duration is usually three or four years and focuses on developing the communication and managerial skills of a student through theoretical and practical training. During the undergraduate level, a student learns accounting, marketing, economics, financial management, human resource management, marketing strategies, business laws, etc., which develop business decision-making capability in a student. Besides, he learns content writing, content development, report writing and content editing. In order to attain more skills in a particular field, normally students prefer to undertake a Master of Business Administration (MBA) degree. Nowadays, even when a student has an engineering degree or specialisation in any other professional course, he opts for MBA to enhance his qualification for a better placement.

If you are inclined towards any business arena, nothing is better than an undergraduate course in business administration.

Eligibility: You must finish 10 + 2 with commerce or humanities subjects with (or without) mathematics. There are no set criteria and even those with a science background can opt for it.

Institutions: All major universities across the country and many university affiliated and private colleges provide courses in business administration.

Placements: Banks, multinational companies, insurance sector, and leading names in the industry could use services to further their business interests.

(3) Banking, Finance and Commerce

There was a time when not many students preferred commerce subjects at senior secondary stage. Brightest students used to opt for science. Now the situation is just the opposite. Even science students in engineering do business management which involves all the possible courses in finance and business. Courses in finance, accounts and banking are to some extent similar areas, but differ in services. Jobs in banking, finance and accounting sectors are exciting and offer excellent opportunities to learn about businesses and interact with people from various fields.

Due to the fact that new and private banks are emerging every now and then, there is vast scope in banking services. For a graduate in banking, there are numerous job opportunities. Banks like American Express, Standard Chartered, Barclay's, ICICI, HSBC, ABN Amro, Kotak Mahindra, HDFC, etc., offer decent salaries at all the levels. A qualified graduate in banking also finds jobs in insurance, mortgages, personal loans, to name a few. For a highly qualified and experienced graduate with a degree from good management colleges, there is a wide scope as an investment banker.

Courses offered:

- Banking
- Taxation
- Financial analysis
- Chartered accountancy
- Insurance
- Cost and work accountancy
- Capital Market
- Forensic accountancy
- Investment banking
- Mutual fund
- Financial planning
- Consultancy

Options in Banking:

- Environment and Management of Financial Services
- Micro Economics
- Effective Banking Communication
- Quantitative Techniques in Banking
- Organizational Behaviour in Banking Organizations
- Taxation of Financial Services
- Laws relating to Banking and Insurance
- Cost Accounting of Banking and Services
- Equity Debt
- Corporate Laws governing Capital Markets
- International Business Management in Banking Organizations

- HRM in Banking Organizations
- Strategic Planning in Banking organizations

Professional Institutes:

1. International College of Financial Planning, New Delhi. Web: www.collegefp.com
2. Association of Financial Planners, Mumbai, Maharashtra. Web: www.afpindia.org
3. Financial Planners & Advisory Academy Pvt Ltd, Mumbai, Maharashtra. www.fpaaacademy.com

Other Institutes:

- NSHM College of Management & Technology, Durgapur Kolkata, West Bengal
- Subash Institute of Business Management, Bangalore, Karnataka
- Adarsh Mahila Mahavidyalaya, Bhiwani, Haryana
- Netaji Subhash Chandra Bose Girls Government Degree College, University of Lucknow, Uttar Pradesh
- School of Business Studies, Sharda University, Greater Noida, Delhi - NCR
- Ghanshyam Das Saraf College of Arts and Commerce, Mumbai, Maharashtra

Placements: Government and private banks, insurance agencies and other multinational companies.

(4) Actuarial Science

Actuarial Science is a branch of science that applies mathematical and statistical methods to assess risks in insurance and finance industries. Those in this field are assigned to work in a wide range of areas like life insurance, general insurance, pensions and employee benefits, health insurance, reinsurance companies, investment, consultancies and risk management. Actuarial services in insurance and pensions are very important for the stability of the financial system and asset-liability valuation of investors. It deals with managing risk for profit of a firm, product pricing, product designing, customer value management, risk and capital management. Those who provide actuarial services are known as actuaries. Actuarial science is also applied to property, casualty, liability, and general insurance.

Actuaries must have skills as a statistician, economist and financier and employ techniques of probability, and must know about details of compound interest, law, marketing and management to predict the outcome of future contingencies and design solutions to lessen the financial severity of such events. The course is globally recognized. The major fields in actuaries are in the life-insurance sector, general insurance, health insurance, pensions and employee benefits, investment consultancies, risk management, banks, stock exchanges, human resource consulting, private and government agencies. This is one field where demand exceeds supply, thereby increasing career prospects in this field.

Eligibility: Actuarial Science has totally different programmes. It is sort of a professional course where graduates and post-graduates can also apply. Those who are already in service can also pursue the courses for improving their lot.

- 10+2 passed students having attained 85% marks in mathematics / statistics
- Graduate or post-graduate students with 55% aggregate or more in mathematics, statistics, econometrics, computer science, and physics.
- CA, MCA, ICWA, CFA, MBA (Finance), Engineers

Courses: B. Sc. (+ M.Sc. Dual Degree)

(1) Actuarial Science (Dual Degree: 5 years)
(2) Insurance & Banking (3 years)
(3) Insurance & Risk Management

Procedure:

In India, a fellow member of the Institute of Actuaries-India (IAI) is known as an actuary. To become a fellow, one has to first become a student member of the institute and then clear all the papers of the institute and fulfil other criteria from time to time. IAI is a statutory body established under The Actuaries Act 2006 (35 of 2006) for regulation of profession of actuaries in India. The provisions of the said Act have come into force from 10 November 2006, in terms of the notification dated 8 November 2006, issued by the Government of India in the Ministry of Finance, Department of Economic Affairs. As a consequence of this, the erstwhile Actuarial Society of India was dissolved and all the assets and liabilities of the Actuarial Society of India were transferred to, and vested in, the Institute of Actuaries of India constituted under Section 3 of the Actuaries Act, 2006.

Duration of Courses:

There are a total of 15 papers: 9 in CT series, 3 in CA series, 2(out of 6) in ST series and 1(out of 6) in SA series. There is no fixed duration of the course. Ideally if pursued dedicatedly, the course could be completed in 3-4 years.

Professional Institutes:

1. Institute of Actuaries of India, Mumbai, Maharashtra
   Web: www.actuariesindia.org
2. International School of Actuarial Sciences in the Institute

of Insurance and Risk Management (ISRM), Hyderabad, Andhra Pradesh
Web: www.iirmworld.org.in
3. Amity School of Insurance and Acturial Science, Noida
Web: www.amity.edu

Placements: Multinational companies, insurance agencies, banks, mobile phone companies, stock exchanges, etc.

(5) Company Secretary

A company secretary is a specialist in Company Law and Corporate Law and is an important string between various government authorities, shareholders and board of directors. He/ she is also a corporate planner and strategic manager. He is also free to take on independent practice. Among his prominent services are: corporate restructuring, tax advisor, financial management, arbitration, project planning, foreign collaboration and joint ventures, auditing, etc. Besides, he is an expert in securities management, banking services, human resource management, public services and international trade.

The Institute of Company Secretaries of India conducts an eight months Foundation Programme after finishing which the candidate is eligible for Executive Programme.

The Institute of Company Secretaries of India (ICSI) functions under the Ministry of Corporate Affairs and its headquarters are situated in New Delhi and regional offices in four metropolitan cities, besides seventy other centres throughout India. Its vision is "to be a global leader in promoting good corporate governance" and its mission "to develop high calibre professionals facilitating good corporate governance". The courses have been designed to develop skills and competence in the field of corporate affairs.

There is provision of 24x7 e-learning programme for which one may log on to http://elearning.icsi.edu.

Eligibility: 10+2 in any stream

Duration: 8 months

Examinations: Twice in a year (1) Registration up to 31 March for December examination (2) Registration up to 30 September for June examination of the next year.

Admission: Open throughout the year

Address: The Institute of Company Secretaries of India, ICSI House, 22 Institutional Area, Lodhi Road, New Delhi – 110 003

6

Science-Based Courses

(1) Environmental Science

Environment, in simplest terms can be summarized as natural life on earth. An environmentalist is someone who works to protect the environment from destruction or pollution. Environmental science is the branch of biology that deals with the relations between organisms, their environment and the solution of environmental problems. It encompasses other fields like ecology, geology, chemistry, physics and atmospheric science.

Due to industrialization, environment is being affected rapidly and there is urgent need of correcting the elements responsible for its constant destruction. Many of the species have disappeared from earth and many more are on the verge of extinction. The responsibility of an environmentalist is to protect our environment from these elements. It is a huge task and unless and until the balance between life and nature is not equated, it cannot be achieved.

Sometime ago, not many people realized the importance of environment in our natural lives. But as species are vanishing, temperature is increasing, glaciers are melting, sea levels are increasing, forests are denuding, and the atmosphere is being polluted, it is the high time to protect our environment. Due to all these problems, the role of an environmentalist is extremely important. This has led to the introduction of environmental science as a subject. Pollution, whether it is air or water or in any other medium, is a global phenomenon as such. Thus, the scope of work and growth in this field is very wide and employment opportunities aplenty.

Scope of Environmental Studies: Industries, management of forest and wildlife, urban planning, pollution control boards, ministry of environment and forests, agriculture and water resources, research and development, NGOs, as a teacher in colleges, and international organisations.

Courses: B. Sc. (Environmental Science)
(One can proceed to do M. Sc. and Ph. D. later)

Professional Institutes:

- Aligarh Muslim University, Uttar Pradesh
- Anna University, Guindy, Chennai, Tamil Nadu
- Awadh University, Faizabad, Uttar Pradesh
- B.R. Ambedkar Marathwada University, Aurangabad, Maharashtra
- Babasaheb Bhimrao Ambedkar University, Agra, Uttar Pradesh
- Chaudhary Charan Singh University, Meerut, Uttar Pradesh
- Delhi College of Engineering, Delhi
- Department of Environmental Biology, Delhi University, Delhi
- GB Pant University of Agriculture and Technology, Pantnagar, Uttar Pradesh
- Guru Gobind Singh Indraprastha University, Delhi
- Guru Jambheshwar University, Hisar, Haryana

- School of Environmental Sciences, Jawahral Nehru University (JNU), New Delhi
- Tamil Nadu Veterinary and Animal Sciences University, Chennai, Tamil Nadu
- University of Jammu, Jammu, Jammu & Kashmir
- University of Madras, Chennai, Tamil Nadu
- University of Mysore, Mysore, Karnataka

Placements:

- Ministry of Environment & Forest
- University Colleges
- Government departments
- TERI (The Energy and Resources Institute), New Delhi
- United Nations Development Programme (UNDP), New Delhi
- The Centre for Science and Environment, New Delhi

(2) **Bioinformatics**

Bioinformatics is an interdisciplinary science where computer technology is applied to biological problems. This combines biology, computer science and information technology. It provides careers for many from the arena of software development, medication development, analyses and web laboratory analyses. It opens ways for biomedical and pharmaceutical sciences, research institutes, hospitals, sequence assembly and analyzing, database design and maintenance and industry. A graduate in Bioinformatics can easily get a job in India and abroad.

The demand for bioinformatics graduates is increasing at a fast pace. As the secrets of the universe are being unravelled by space research, so are the secrets of life by bioinformatics. The Human Genome Project has created so much of data that the scientists in Bioinformatics will take a decade to analyse them. The discovery of DNA by the trio Watson, Crick and Wilkins some decades ago has generated new avenues for exciting research. The DNA of all living organisms has the same structure in human beings, plants, animals and micro-organisms, some of their genes can be transported from the cells of one organism to another cell to give new shapes and traits to individuals.

There are two aspects of bioinformatics: development of software and methods to employ the same. An aspirant to set career in bioinformatics must have knowledge of physics, chemistry, biology, computer science, mathematics and statistics so that he/she may develop new algorithms for implementation of computer programs for biological data analysis and displaying the results. Bioinformatics also plays an important role in areas like functional genomics, structural genomics, and proteomics, and forms a key component in the biotechnology and pharmaceutical sector.

Eligibility: 10+2 with science subjects

The selection of the candidate will depend on marks obtained in 10+2 or entrance examination, as specified by institutes.

Undergraduate Courses

- B.Sc. in Biotechnology
- B.Sc. (Hos.) in Biotechnology
- B.E/B.Tech

Professional Institutes: Renowned colleges and universities across India offer a degree course in bioinformatics. Some of them are listed herewith:

1. Amity Institute of Biotechnology, Amity Campus, Noida
   Web: www.amity.edu/aib
2. Institute of Bioinformatics and Applied Biotechnology, Bangalore, Karnataka
   Web: www. ibab.ac.in

3. DAV College Chandigarh, Chandigarh
   Web: www.davchd.com

Other Institutes:

- Pondicherry University, Puducherry
- Sardar Patel University, Gujarat
- University of Calcutta, West Bengal
- University of Delhi, Delhi
- Jamia Millia Islamia University, Delhi

Placements: Well-known names in the industry – Accenture, Biocon, Carl Zeiss, GlaxoSmithKline, Mphasis, TCS – employ graduates from this discipline. One could also try working with research institutes, hospitals and laboratories as scientist and at universities.

(3) Biotechnology

Biotechnology is a technology based on biology. Basically it has applications in many areas that include health care, crop production, better variety of food and protection of environment. It helps improve our lives by providing vaccines to save millions of lives and preventing rare and untreated diseases as also reducing rates of infectious diseases and creating tools for the detection of diseases. In the field of medicine, it has found applications in drug production, pharmaceuticals, genomics, gene therapy, genetic screening to detect genetic diseases, etc. It encompasses diverse areas of study like molecular biology, tissue culture, agricultural engineering, fisheries, genetics or even medicine.

In the agriculture sector, biotechnology is used to increase yields, preventing damage from insects and pests and improving crop insect resistance. Because of Biotechnology, farmers are using less pesticide on their crops so as to reduce soil tillage. Through this technology, drought-resistant crops are being developed which enable agricultural production to withstand adverse growing conditions. It is creating biodegradable plastics made from renewable sources. These plastics are versatile and help us reduce our use of petrochemicals.

Biotechnology plays a fundamental role in developing sustainable solutions for many of today's most critical environmental concerns. Biotech breakthroughs help reduce air emissions and water pollution while enabling the development of sustainable, earth-friendly products. Biotechnology helps reducing our environmental problems, generating processes cleaner and more efficient by reducing toxic chemical pollution and greenhouse gas emissions. Due to high population rate, biotechnology industry has a big scope in India.

Besides, biotechnologists find jobs in the research laboratories, research and development centres, pharmaceutical companies, and agricultural, chemical and allied industries, animal husbandry, medicine, crime and parentage disputes, cell biology, ecology, soil conservation science, physiology of plants, biostatistics, forestry and fisheries, etc. Biotechnology is ranked second as a growth sector after multimedia industry with a tremendous employment potential.

Eligibility: 10+2 with science including Biology / Agriculture

Undergraduate Courses: A biotechnology course includes a (B.Sc./B.Tech.) degree in Biochemistry, Genetics, Microbiology, Chemistry, Virology, Immunology and Engineering.

Professional Institutions: Biotechnology as an undergraduate course is taught in almost every university of India. Some of these are mentioned below:

- Indian Institute of Technology (Chennai; Guwahati; Kharagpur; Roorkee)

- Motilal Nehru National Institute of Technology, Allahabad
- National Institute of Technology (Calicut; Durgapur; Raipur)
- Kurukshetra University, Haryana
- Lovely Professional University (LPU), Punjab
- Maharshi Dayanand University, Haryana
- Sardar Vallabh Bhai Patel University of Agriculture & Technology, Uttar Pradesh
- Thapar University, Punjab

Placements: Centres for cellular and molecular biology, research institutes, botanical institutes, laboratories, etc.

(4) Microbiology

Microbiology is the branch of biology that deals with the structure, function, uses, and modes of existence of microscopic organisms and their effects on other living organisms. It encompasses numerous sub-disciplines including virology, mycology, parasitology, and bacteriology. As pure microbiology, it encompasses the study of protozoa, bacteria, fungi, algae, viruses, microbes, nematodes, parasites, and immune system.

Apart from pure microbiology, it also includes microbial growth, microbial metabolism and microbial cell structure, the relationship between microorganisms and their environment, micro genetics, cellular microbiology, the study of the evolution of microbes, the study of the genetic relationship of micro-organisms, etc., the study of microorganisms in outer space and the microorganisms on nano level.

There is a wrong notion that micro-organisms are responsible for deadly diseases only. It has many benefits like production of antibiotics, yeast, curd, alcohol, vinegar, vitamins, amino acids and many dairy products. These minute organisms are beneficial in biodegradation of toxic, industrial and domestic wastes also. Micro-organisms also help in aiding digestion.

A student pursuing microbiology at undergraduate level can work in industries like breweries, distilleries, dairy farms, pharmaceutical among many others. Candidates can also pursue post-graduate courses to get better jobs. If he/she is interested in teaching or research work, it is essential to pursue the Ph.D. programme. There are various certificate, diploma and short-term courses in different disciplines of microbiology for jobs at the beginner and intermediate levels. There are specialisation courses in many fields of microbiology like bacteriology, virology, immunology, applied microbiology, microbial biotechnology, medical microbiology, food and dairy microbiology, veterinary and agricultural microbiology, etc.

Eligibility: 10+2 with science including biology / agriculture

Undergraduate Courses: A microbiology course (B.Sc./B.Tech.) includes study in biochemistry, genetics, microbiology, chemistry, virology, immunology and engineering.

Professional Institutions: Microbiology at undergraduate course is taught in almost every university of India. Some of these are mentioned below:

- Institute of Home Economics, University of Delhi, Delhi
- St. Josephs College, Benguluru, Karnataka
- St. Xavier's College, Mumbai, Maharashtra
- Manipal Academy of Higher Education, Karnataka
- Indira Priyadarshini Degree College for Women, Hyderabad, Andhra Pradesh
- St. Francis College for Women, Hyderabad, Andhra Pradesh

- Barkatullah Vishwavidyalaya, Bhopal, Madhya Pradesh
- G.H.G. Khalsa College, Ludhiana, Punjab
- Aligarh Muslim University, Uttar Pradesh
- Presidency College, Kolkata, West Bengal

(5) **Petroleum and Energy Studies**

Oil, gas and power are the backbones of any country for its development. It is easy to operate any domestic machine that requires electric power or a gas stove in the kitchen, but to produce such user-friendly appliances require tremendous amount of expertise. Besides these, there are other projects concerning transportation, information technology, aviation, port and shipping, and logistics and supply chain. The University of Petroleum and Energy Studies (UPES), based in Dehradun fulfils these requirements and offers B. Tech programmes in various fields of engineering. This is Asia's first energy and core sector university. These highly specialised contemporary programmes aim to meet the industry requirements for the next two decades and its graduates are offered lucrative jobs.

Courses:

(i) **B. Tech (Fire & Safety Engineering)**

Job Categories:

* Fire & Safety Engineer
* Safety Officer
* Safety Engineer
* Manager / Advisor – Fire & Safety
* Health, Safety & Environment Engineer
* Industrial Fire & Safety Engineer
* Fire & Safety Consultant
* Fire & Safety Faculty in Educational Institutions

(ii) B. Tech (Core Engineering Sectors)

* Applied Petroleum Engineering
* Chemical Engineering
* Geo Science Engineering
* Aerospace Engineering
* Geo Informatics Engineering
* Automotive Design Engineering
* Electronics Engineering
* Mechatronics Engineering
* Power System Engineering
* Civil Engineering
* Computer Science Engineering

(iii) Techno-Legal Programmes

* Energy Technology + LLB with specialization in intellectual property rights (5-year course)
* Computer Science + specialization in Cyber Law.

(iv) BBA Programmes

* Oil & Gas Marketing
* Aviation Operations
* Logistic Management
* Auto Marketing

Eligibility: Minimum 60 % marks at 10 +2 or equivalent (PCM)
Admission criteria: UPES Engineering Aptitude Test followed by centralised counselling.

(6) Architecture

Nowadays the word 'builder' has become very popular. Basically a builder is an architect who by profession designs buildings and environments with an element of aesthetics. Architecture is the art and science of designing buildings and other physical structures.

This is one of the oldest professions in the world which can be gauged from the historical structures, forts, temples, churches, mosques, bridges, roads which have artistically pleasing designs. With the growth of economy in India, not only the big cities but small towns also require the services of architects to design the structures in pleasing ways.

In order to join an under-graduate course in architecture (B. Arch), the basic qualification is class XII with physics, chemistry, and mathematics. Besides good grades at +2 level, an aspiring student in this field should have an artistic taste because constructing buildings of any sort would require novelty and beauty. He should possess creativity, keen observation, knowledge of building material, urban conservation, heritage management and of course skill in drawing and sketching. Lutyen's Delhi, Chandigarh, Lotus Temple, etc are examples of originality and aesthetics.

The job of an architect is not only to design houses; it also involves many other things like rural or urban planning, landscape designing, interior designing, etc. He has to update his knowledge about latest developments in the field of architecture. When a big task is ahead, he should have a burning desire to know the history of the place and events keeping in view the future requirements.

There is a great demand of architects in India because of rapid development in infrastructure in urban and rural towns. With experience and skill, one may rise to senior posts with very high incomes pretty soon. For a practicing architect, the biggest scope is in real estate. An architect can work independently or join some government or private organization. Some government agencies are Public Works Department (PWD), the Archaeological Department, Public Sector Undertakings, Housing and Urban Development Corporation, National Building Organization, National Institute of Urban Affairs, and many others.

Undergraduate courses

• The School of Planning and Architecture, New Delhi. It is a specialized university, the only one of its kind, which exclusively provides training at various levels, in different aspects of human habitat and environment. It provides courses for under-graduates, post-graduates, and doctoral level. The selection of admission will be based on performance in the qualifying examination and interview.

Eligibility criteria: 10 + 2 or equivalent in any stream

Undergraduate Courses:

* B. Arch. (5 years)
* Bachelor of Planning (B. Plan) (4 years)

Professional Institutes:

1. School of Planning and Architecture, Delhi
   Web: www.spa.ac.in
2. KR Mangalam University, Delhi-NCR
   Web: www. krmangalam.edu.in
3. Ansal University, Gurgaon, Haryana
   Web: www.ansaluniversity.edu.in
4. Chandigarh University, Chandigarh
   Web: www.chandigarhuniversity.ac.in
5. Sharda University, Delhi
   Web: www.sharda.ac.in
6. Lovely Professional University, Punjab
   Web: www.lpu.in

(7) **Forensic Sciences**

Forensic Sciences or Forensics is a very wide branch of science which basically deals with scientific support and services to the investigation of crime. But this is not the only function of Forensics. It covers other fields such as astronomy, archaeology, biology, and geology to investigate ancient times including identification of skeletonized human or animals remains. The specialists in this field analyze and investigate the elements like dead bodies and tissues, to find out the identities of such elements employing modern technologies. It is a sort of research work that is performed in the laboratories.

The range of topics in forensics covers almost all the subjects including computational forensics, ballistics, firearms and tool mark examinations, and other evidences in criminal investigations, medicine, pathology, toxicology, profiling, imaging, policing, anthropology, archaeology, entomology, genetics, digital forensics, forensic chemistry, forensic dactyloscopy (the study of fingerprints), forensic engineering, forensic geophysics, forensic meteorology, forensic limnology (the analysis of evidence collected from crime scenes), forensic odontology (study of teeth), forensic podiatry (the study of feet footprint), forensic toxicology, and many other fields.

Eligibility: 10 + 2 with science subjects

Undergraduate courses:

- B. Sc. (Forensic Sciences)
- Advanced Diploma, Diploma, and Certificate Courses (3 to 12 months)

Job Profile in Forensics:

- Forensic Investigator
- Document Examiner
- Investigating Officer
- Handwriting Expert
- Fingerprint Expert

- Genetics Expert
- Forensic Psychologist
- Government and Private Detective
- Forensic Consultant

Professional Institutes:

1. Gujarat Forensic Sciences University, Gujarat
   Web: www.gfsu.edu.in
2. National Institute of Criminology and Forensic Science, Delhi
   Web: www.nicfs.nic.in
3. Institute of Forensic Science, Nagpur, Maharashtra
   Web: www.ifscnagpur.in

Placements: Police departments, Central Bureau of Investigation (CBI), Central and State Forensic Sciences Laboratories, Criminal Investigation Department (CID), Intelligence Bureau (IB), Quality Control Bureau, narcotics departments, hospitals, courts, and university colleges.

(8) Nutrition and Dietetics

For quite some time, educated people in urban India have become diet-conscious because diet plays a major role in promotion of health and well-being of an individual. Look at the figures of film stars and models! They are so slim and full of energy because they understand the value of being fit; that also enables them to perform better. A good and balanced diet habit improves the quality of life while poor diet may lead to a number of diseases including obesity. Nutritionists and dietetics deal with this aspect. Dietetics is the science and art of feeding individuals based on the principles of nutrition. While dietetics is related to food management, nutrition is related to promotion of health.

You must have seen diabetic people concerned about their diet. Similarly, senior citizens also have a simple diet – one or two *chapatis*, fresh vegetables and lots of fruits. Even young people, especially women, avoid fats and carbohydrates. Indian people are also understanding the role of nutritionists and dieticians in improving the quality of their life.

Because of their specialisation in healthy and nutritious diet-planning, the nutritionists and dieticians get absorbed easily in government and private hospitals, nursing homes, boarding schools, fitness centres, five-star hotels, sports and health clubs, and also in research institutes. International organisations like UNO, UNICEF, FAO, etc., also employ them.

Career options in Nutrition and Dietetics:

(a) Clinical Nutritionist/ Dieticians: These specialists in consultation with doctors make plans for the food intake of patients in hospitals and nursing homes and monitor their progress.

(b) Community Nutritionist/ Dieticians: Government and private agencies hire them to take care of the health of people, young and old, who go to fitness clubs and gymnasiums. They also serve in day-care centres for children. Through lectures, demonstrations and meetings, they give useful health-care tips to the public.

(c) Consultant Nutritionist/ Dieticians: These specialists work independently and usually give counselling to rich people and VIPs like film stars and other celebrities. They are much in demand in fitness and sports clubs, spas, 5-star hotels, etc.

(d) Management Nutritionist/ Dieticians: They plan and design nutritious food programmes for children and employees in boarding schools, multi-national companies, private organizations and hospitals, respectively.

Eligibility: 10+2 in science with Biology / Home Science from any recognised board.

Undergraduate courses:

- B. Sc. (Clinical Nutrition, Dietetics and Catering Management)
- B. Sc. (Food Science Management)
- B. Sc. (Dietetics and Applied Nutrition)
- B. Sc. (Nutrition and Dietetics)
- Diploma courses

A graduate can further pursue M. Sc. and Ph. D.

Professional Institutes:

- National Institute of Nutrition, Hyderabad, Andhra Pradesh
- Institute of Home Economics, Delhi University, Delhi
- Lady Irwin College, Delhi University, Delhi
- Acharya NG Ranga Agriculture University, Hyderabad, Andhra Pradesh
- Women's Christian College, Chennai, Tamil Nadu
- University of Mumbai, Mumbai, Maharashtra
- Maharaja Syajiro University of Baroda, Vadodara, Gujarat
- St. Teresa's College, Ernakulam, Kerala
- Maharana Pratap University of Agriculture and Technology, Udaipur, Rajasthan
- Christian Medical College, Vellore, Tamil Nadu
- Sri Ramachandra University, Chennai, Tamil Nadu.

Placements: Government hospitals, government's health department, schools, colleges, and office cafeterias, sports and health clubs, private hospitals and clinics, research and development, food and beverage companies

(9) Allied Health Sciences / Health Care Industry

Health sciences and public health deal with the study of health, disease and the factors affecting them. Government and private hospitals around the world and international health agencies like World Health Organisation (WHO) are promoting the well-being of general public through health care programmes to prevent diseases and improve the quality of life. The human longevity is increased due to such programmes and people are being educated about health care. Deadly disease like smallpox has been completely eradicated from the world long back and polio is on the brink of being eradicated.

Trained, primary and supportive healthcare workers and paramedical staff are required in the health sector from local community to a large-scale population. As health care is necessary for all human beings, the health science workers are always in demand. Since it is a worldwide necessity, it has rather become one of the world's largest and fastest-growing industries. In small communities, there are government dispensaries which provide medicines and consultations free of cost. Due to publicity and advertisements, even the uneducated lot get aware of the health programmes, especially the polio immunisation and other vaccinations to the children.

Eligibility: 10+2 in science with minimum 50% marks in physics, chemistry, biology and / or mathematics. (In some courses. Medical Laboratory Technology Diploma holders can also apply).

Undergraduate courses:

- Optometry (3 years + 1 year Clinical Experience)
- Clinical Laboratory Science (CLS)
- Food Science and Nutrition
- Dialysis Technology

- Nuclear Medicine Technology
- Operation Theatre and Anaesthesia Technology
- Radiology and Imaging Technology
- Paramedical Science Diploma
- Diploma in Clinical Echo Cardiography
- Diploma in Dialysis Technology

Professional Institutes:

1. Mother Teresa Institute of Postgraduate and Research Institute of Health Sciences, Puducherry
   Web: www.mtihs.puducherry.gov.in
2. ITN Institute of Health Sciences (SNDT University affiliated, Government of Maharashtra approved courses), Maharashtra
   Web: www.sndt.in
3. MIOT Academy of Allied Health Sciences, Chennai, Tamil Nadu
   Web: www.miot_aahs.com
4. School of Allied Health Sciences (SOAHS), Manipal, Karnataka
   Web: www.manipal.edu

Placements: Banks, hospitals, multi-national companies, NGOS, clinics, acadenic institites, etc.

(10) Home Science

Home science can be defined as "education for better living". The objective is meant for prosperous living and achieving the highest happiness. It encompasses both art and science. Home science essentially deals with different aspects of housekeeping. The objective is to foster the growth, development and wellbeing of individual's families and communities, utilising the findings and advances of science and technology. It is a need-based, professionally-course oriented to assist family and community towards improved living. Home science education tries to create an environment and outlook, which will enable people to live richer and more purposeful lives. It tries to provide a wholesome knowledge and right attitude towards family health (both physical and psychological), nutrition, child care, home decoration, elderly care and management during risk and eventualities. It tries further to enrich the lives of each and every member of the family through better understanding of the human relationships.

Home Science in Indian universities is a recognised subject. Since it is a specialised course, there is much demand at the undergraduate and post-graduate levels.

Eligibility 10+2 examination with science subjects such as biology, math and chemistry. The duration for this course is 3 years.

Undergraduate courses:

- B.Sc. (Home Science)
- B. Sc. (Household Science)
- B. Sc. (Home Science & Nutrition)
- Diploma in Home Science
- Advanced Diploma in Child Guidance and Family Counselling

Specialized fields:

- Home Management
- Household Science
- Child Development
- Extension Education
- Foods and Nutrition
- Clothing and Textiles

Professional Institutes:

- Department of Home Science, Institute of Home Economics, University of Delhi
  Web: www.du.ac.in
- A.V. Kamalamma College for Women, Bangalore, Karnataka
- Acharya N.G. Ranga Agricultural University, Hyderabad, Andhra Pradesh
- Adharshila College of Education, Meerut, Uttar Pradesh
- Angul Mahila Mahavidyalaya (AMM), Odisha

Placements:

- Teaching in schools and colleges
- Research assistants; Junior Research Fellow
- Therapeutic dietician
- Field supervisors
- Food preservation
- Interior decorator
- Counsellors
- Hospitals
- International agencies like UNICEF, CARE, NIPCCD, World Bank
- NGOs
- Welfare organizations
- Apparel merchandising
- Restaurants and cafeterias

(11) Veterinary Science

Veterinary Science is a branch of science dealing with diagnosing diseases in animals, birds, domestic pets, poultries and livestock and then treating and curing the same. This also includes care of animal health as well as animal husbandry and handling of livestock. Veterinary doctors also perform surgery of animals if required, besides administrating necessary vaccinations from time to time for preventing and spreading the diseases to other animals.

The job of a veterinary doctor is not that easy, because he cannot ask an animal 'what he has eaten'! Unlike human beings, he cannot direct the animal to do what the doctor wants. For this purpose, he requires to know the behaviour and characteristics of animals which vary from animal to animal. He must know the anatomy of animals. A vet should have love and compassion for animals to stay in this profession.

A qualified veterinary doctor is much in demand, especially in metropolitan cities as people here are fond of pets. They are required in government and private hospitals besides in zoos and national parks, zoo, poultry and animal farms, dairy farms, race clubs, mounted regiments in army, and government animal husbandry departments. Some have private clinics like dog's clinic.

Eligibility: 10 + 2 with science subjects

(Veterinary Council of India conducts an 'All India Entrance Examination'

Undergraduate courses:

Duration of course is 4 ½ to 5 years.

- Bachelor's degree in Veterinary Science (B.V.Sc.)
- Bachelor's degree in Veterinary Science and Animal Husbandry (B.V.Sc.& AH)
- Bachelor of Veterinary Science (Animal Genetics and Breeding)
- Bachelor of Science (Animal Production Management)

Professional Institutions:

- Rajiv Gandhi Institute of Veterinary Education and Research, Puducherry
  Web: www.ragacovas.com
- College of Veterinary Science and Animal Husbandry, Mhow, Madhya Pradesh
  Web: www.mppcvv.org
- Department of Animal Science, Mahatma Jyotiba Phule Rohilkhand University, Bareilly, Uttar Pradesh
  Web: www.mjpru.ac.in
- College of Veterinary Science and Animal Husbandry, Junagadh Agricultural University, Junagadh, Gujarat
- Khalsa College of Veterinary and Animal Sciences, Amritsar, Punjab
- Sri Ganganagar Veterinary College, Rajasthan
- Faculty of Veterinary Science and Animal Husbandry, Birsa Agricultural University, Ranchi, Jharkhand
- College of Veterinary Sciences and Animal Husbandry, Central Agricultural University, Mizoram
- Department of Animal Nutrition, West Bengal University of Animal and Fishery Sciences, Kolkata, West Bengal
- Department of Animal Production and Management, West Bengal University of Animal and Fishery Sciences, Kolkata, West Bengal

Placement: Veterinary assistants, veterinary surgeons, veterinary scientists, specialist veterinarians, animal clinics, zoological parks, academics.

(12) Merchant Navy

Merchant Navy is the commercial fleet of non-combatant ships dealing with the transportation of cargo and passengers. Though you spend the major part of your life on ships where you come across too many problems, but at the end you are the winner by accumulating a lot of money. If you like adventures and want to see the world without spending money, then Merchant Navy must be your choice.

India has one of the largest merchant shipping fleets that includes passenger ships, cargo ships, container ships, tanker ships, etc. Merchant Navy is a highly professional and technologically advanced industry. It is a peaceful global body which is into transportation of goods and people, comprises passenger vessels, cargo, cruise liners, and other specialized ships to carry goods from one country to another.

You must be acquainted with what job you will be holding on the ships. There are various departments which are assigned important duties on the ships. The in charge of the ship is called 'Captain' who is responsible for the navigation and safety of passengers, crew and cargo. The officers in the Deck department look for the maintenance of the ship's hull and safety of the equipment.

Every ship has a captain or master who is in charge of the ship. He is responsible for the navigation, discipline and the safety of the passengers, crew and cargo. He must ensure the observance of national and international codes of conduct. The marine engineers of the engine department operate and maintain navigational systems and ensure functioning on the technical parts of the vessel. The Service department does the remaining tasks like catering and providing necessary services.

Eligibility Class X or XII with science subjects. Age limit: 16 to 25 years

Entry: The All India Merchant Navy Entrance Test (AIMNET) is conducted by Bharat Shipping Limited in various courses like Nautical Science and Marine Engineering usually in November or December. Only unmarried males and females are eligible.

Undergraduate courses:

- B.Sc. (Nautical Science)
- B. Sc. (Nautical Technology)
- B. E. (Marine Engineering)
- B. Tech (Naval Architecture and Ship Building)
- B. Tech (Marine Engineering)

Professional Institutes:

1. Tolani Maritime Institute, Mumbai, Maharashtra
   Web: www.tolani.edu/tmi/
2. Samundra Institute of Maritime Studies, Maharashtra
   Web: www.samundra.com
3. International Maritime Institute, Greater Noida, Uttar Pradesh
   Web: www.imi.edu
4. Maharashtra Academy of Naval Education and Training, Pune, Maharashtra
   Web: www.manetpune.com
5. Indian Maritime University, Chennai, Tamil Nadu
   Web: www.imu.edu.in

7
Agriculture-Based Courses

(1) Agriculture

Earlier it was thought that agriculture is confined to farmers living in rural areas only, especially in the Indian context. But this field of career has enormous potential so far as agricultural commodities like flowers, spices, cereals, oilseeds and vegetables are concerned. Food is the first and foremost requirement of human beings and it has become a highly profitable business. Due to scientific researches in this field, there is tremendous scope in both academics and other areas.

Since India is one of the largest producers of agricultural products like vegetables and fruits, it has attracted the attention of exporters who supply these commodities on global scale. Due to continuous scientific researches in agriculture field, new varieties of food stuff are emerging every now and then. An agriculture scientist is involved in research to design the production and processing of food products like meats, fish, and varieties of dairy products. If you visit a modern store in your area, you will find hundreds of varieties of biscuits and other eatables. Its importance can be gauged from the fact that maximum number of shops in any market belong to items connected with food, including eateries.

The job opportunities in the agriculture field can be summarised as; production and supply of vegetables and fruits; dairy products; horticulture and floriculture; exports of flowers, spices, cereals; plant pathology; breeding of domesticated animals; botany; entomology; agronomy; bacteriology; soil chemistry; seed production; and of course, in academics.

Indian Council of Agriculture Research (ICAR) and agriculture universities are the main agencies to produce and recruit graduates for further research in this field. After doing B. Sc. in agriculture, one can get jobs in poultry and breeding farms, seed companies, nurseries, agribusiness, forestry, fishery, beautification of surroundings in holiday resorts, health farms and hotels through landscapes and horticulture.

Eligibility: 10+2 with science subjects from any recognised board

Entrance exams: Indian Council of Agriculture Research (ICAR) conducts an all India entrance examination for admission to undergraduate programme in agricultural and allied subjects. The entrance exam for undergraduate admissions consists of only one question paper with objective type questions. The question paper is bilingual i.e. English and Hindi.

- For stream A, the subject composition is Physics, Chemistry, Biology / Agriculture.
- For stream B, the subject combination is Physics, Chemistry and Mathematics.

Undergraduate courses:

- B.Sc. in Agriculture: (4-years)
- B.Sc. (Hons.) in Agriculture: (3-years)
- Diploma course in Agriculture (2-years)
- Certificate Course in Agriculture Science: (1-year) after Class X

Those who are selected, the following undergraduate programmes are offered in many of the state agricultural universities:

- Agriculture
- Agricultural Engineering
- Horticulture
- Fishery
- Forestry
- Home Science
- Sericulture
- Dairy Technology
- Food Science and Technology
- Agricultural Marketing
- Banking and Co-operation

For further details, contact:

Indian Council of Agricultural Research
Web: www.icar.org.in

A few well-known agriculture universities in India:

1. Acharya N.G. Ranga Agricultural University (ANGRAU), Hyderabad, Andhra Pradesh
2. Anand Agricultural University, Anand, Gujarat
3. Assam Agricultural University (AAU), Jorhat, Assam
4. Birsa Agricultural University (BAU), Ranchi, Jharkhand
5. Central Agricultural University (CAU), Imphal, Manipur
6. Central Institute on Fisheries Education, Mumbai, Maharashtra
7. Dr. Yashwant Singh Parmar University of Horticulture & Forestry, Himachal Pradesh
8. Govind Ballabh Pant University of Agriculture and Technology, Pantnagar, Uttar Pradesh

9. Indian Agricultural Research Institute, New Delhi
10. Indira Gandhi Krishi Vishwa Vidyalaya (IGKVV), Raipur, Chhattisgarh
11. Jawaharlal Nehru Krishi Vishwa Vidyalaya(JNKVV), Jabalpur, Madhya Pradesh
12. Junagadh Agricultural University (JAU), Junagadh, Gujarat
13. Maharana Pratap University of Agriculture & Technology (MPUAT), Udaipur, Rajasthan
14. Punjab Agricultural University, Ludhiana, Punjab
15. Sher-e-Kashmir University of Agricultural Sciences and Technology, Jammu & Kashmir
16. West Bengal University of Animal & Fishery Sciences, Kolkata, West Bengal

(2) Dairy Farming

Dairy farming deals with various technologies involving milk and its products. Besides processing, storage, packaging, transportation and distribution, dairy industry also concerns with raising and breeding cattle. Due to scientific researches and modern technologies, the dairy sector has emerged to be one of the profitable professions for present day youths.

There are numerous milk products, some of them being produced in Indian subcontinent for centuries like *ghee, dahi, mattha* (buttermilk), *lassi, paneer, malai, kulfi, chhena, khoa, shrikhand* and various types of sweets. In fact, India is the largest producer of milk in the world. Due to mechanization and automation of operations coupled with scientific researches, people all over the world enjoy broad range of milk products like cheese, cottage cheese, condensed milk, butter, yogurt, powdered milk, ice cream, custard, infant formula, quark, etc.

Milk and milk products come in the category of 'most wanted food'; there is growing demand of young people to be inducted in this industry. Some years ago, milk production was a local issue and unorganised. Now it is well organised and attracting the youths and entrepreneurs for research, especially after Dr. Verghese Kurien's white revolution in India. There is tremendous scope for large scale commercial dairy farming in India.

From hand-milking to fully automated robotic milking, the dairy technology has made tremendous progress. India is producing world-class milk products. Now consumers prefer branded products instead of homemade ones. Brands like Britannia, Nestle, Cadbury, etc., are very well in demand.

Management of dairy industry requires sound knowledge of selection, breeding and rearing of milk producing animals, and livestock production, besides modern technologies applied in this sector. Knowledge of bacteriology, biochemistry, nutrition, health care of animals, genetics and chemistry is equally desirable. Presently dairy industry is worth ₹ 15,000 crore, curtsey brand name Amul owned by Gujarat Cooperative Milk Marketing Federation (GCMMF). In Gujarat itself, nearly 117 lakhs kilogram of milk was procured a day in 2013 so far. Apart from Gujarat, other states of India are also procuring milk to a great extent, especially Haryana, Uttar Pradesh, Bihar, Maharashtra and Madhya Pradesh. If present day youth think of potentialities of dairy technology, it is not difficult to get lucrative employment after getting degrees and training from agricultural universities spread over India. The National Dairy Development Board (NDDB) is facilitating training programme for dairy farming. There are numerous agricultural universities and institutes in India offering courses in dairy technology, dairy farming and dairy management.

Essential qualifications:

For pursuing undergraduate course in dairy farming, a candidate requires a minimum 55% marks in 10 + 2 with chemistry, physics, mathematics, biology and English as subjects studied. Admission shall be made on the basis of merit through All India Entrance Examination conducted by the Education Division, Indian Council of Agricultural Research, New Delhi. In many institutions, the eligibility for admission to most of these courses is on merit basis. Some institutes conduct entrance tests. The duration of the courses ranges from two to four-and-a-half years, although most courses are of four-year duration.

Undergraduate courses:

- B.Sc. in Agriculture: (4-year course)
- B.Sc. (Hons.) in Agriculture (3-year course)
- Diploma course in Agriculture (2-year course)
- Certificate Course in Agriculture Science (1-year) after Class X
- B. Sc. / B. Tech (Dairy Technology; Agriculture)
- B.VSc. (Bachelor of Veterinary Science and Animal Husbandry)

Employment opportunities (at the following bodies):

- The National Dairy Development Board (NDDB)
- Delhi Milk Scheme
- Gujarat Co-operative Milk Marketing Federation (GCMMF)
- Heritage Foods India Ltd
- Anand Milk Union Limited (Amul)
- Gopaljee Dairy Foods Pvt Ltd
- Dairy Craft India Pvt Ltd

After doing graduation course in dairy related subjects, further qualifications (Master's, Ph.D.) enhance the chances of getting better jobs, particularly in management sectors. Specialisation can be in various fields of dairy technology: dairy technology, dairy chemistry, dairy microbiology, dairy engineering, dairy extension education, food technology, genetics and breeding, dairy quality control, animal biotechnology, livestock production and management, dairy production, and many others.

Proofessional Institutions:

- National Dairy Research Institute (Deemed University), Karnal, Haryana
- National Dairy Research Institute, Bangalore, Karnataka
- Sheth MC College of Dairy Sciences, Anand, Gujarat
- Dairy Science Institute, Mumbai, Maharashtra
- College of Dairy Sciences, Udaipur, Rajasthan
- Dairy Science Institute, Mumbai, Maharashtra
- Jawaharlal Nehru Krishi Vishwavidyalaya, Jabalpur, Madhya Pradesh
- Kerala Agricultural University (College of Veterinary and Animal Sciences), Thrissur
- National Dairy Research Institute, Indian Council of Agricultural Research, Karnal, Haryana
- Rajasthan Agricultural University, College of Dairy Science, Udaipur, Rajasthan
- West Bengal University of Animal and Fishery Sciences, West Bengal

Placements: following companies hire dairy experts on a large scale:

* Almarai Company
* Britannia Industries
* ITC
* Mehsana Dist. Co-op. Milk Union

* Bihar Co-op. Milk Federation
* Nestle India
* SRIJAN India
* Amul
* Delhi Milk Scheme

(3) Fishery Sciences

As the name reflects, fishery is concerned with fishes. Fishery is an important field of agriculture. It has become a science because of modern techniques that enable people in this business not only in catching but breeding, fish processing, freezing, and canning fishes. This includes not only fishes but other varieties of aquatic animals used as sea foods. It is a multi-disciplinary science that includes aquaculture, genetics, biotechnology, microbiology, physiology and fishery environment.

There is wide scope in fishery sciences as sea foods are very popular throughout the world. Fishes constitute almost 70% of seafood consumed the world over and has become a very big industry that requires professionals. Further, fishery is the source of livelihood for many people. India has a long seacoast line and can be used to generate lot of revenue through fishery science education. Presently, most work is done by fishermen but if qualified graduates step in, the production will be very high. Fishery science has a huge export potential and is a big source of foreign exchange earnings for any country.

It is a specialized science and graduates get employment easily. There is big scope in foreign countries like USA, Canada, Australia, Japan, China, European countries, Gulf and African countries.

Essential Qualifications: 10+2 with science subjects

Undergraduate courses:

- B.Sc. in Agriculture: (4-year couse)
- B.Sc. (Hons.) in Agriculture (3-year course)
- Diploma course in Agriculture (2-year course)
- Certificate Course in Agriculture Science (1-year) after Class X
- Bachelor of Fisheries Science (B.F.Sc) (4-years course)

Opportunities:

Most of the graduates are absorbed in State or Central Government departments apart from academic field.

- Inspector of Fisheries/Research Assistants
- Assistant Fisheries Development Officer (AFDO)
- Fisheries Development Officer(FDO)
- Fisheries Managers
- Project Officers
- Fisheries Officers
- Farm Managers
- Hatchery Managers

Professional Institutions:

- Maharana Pratap University of Agriculture and Technology, Udaipur, Rajasthan
- Karnataka Veterinary Animal and Fisheries Sciences University, Mangalore, Karnataka
- Tamil Nadu Fisheries University, Tamil Nadu
- Kerala University of Fisheries and Ocean Studies, Panangad, Kerala
- Dr. Balasaheb Sawant Konkan Krishi Vidyapeeth, Ratnagiri, Maharastra
- West Bengal University of Animal and Fishery Sciences, Kolkata, West Bengal

- Maharashtra Animal & Fishery Sciences University, Nagpur, Maharastra
- Narendra Deva University of Agriculture and Technology, Faizabad, Uttar Pradesh
- Punjab Agriculture University, Ludhiana, Punjab

Placements:

- Research Assistant in colleges, fishery sciences, State Fisheries Development Corporations
- Fish Farmers Development Agency (FFDA)
- Technical officers in Marine Product Export Development Authority (MPEDA)
- Coastal Aquaculture Authority of India (CAA)
- Food Safety and Standards Authority of India (FSSAI)
- Fisheries Survey of India (FSI)
- National Institute of Oceanography(NIO)
- Indian National Centre for Ocean and Information Services(INCOIS)

(4) Horticulture

Horticulture Science deals with plant cultivation which has many diverse activities. Horticulture is a branch of agriculture and its crops include trees, bushes and perennial vine fruits; vegetables like roots, tubers, shoots, stems, leaves, fruits and flowers of edible and mainly annual plants; aromatic and medicinal foliage; seeds and roots; cut flowers, potted ornamental plants, bedding plants and ornamental grasses; and production and marketing of floral crops. It has a vital role in establishing nurseries for use in landscaping or for establishing fruit orchards.

Horticulture involves five areas of study. These areas are floriculture (includes production and marketing of floral crops), landscape horticulture (includes production, marketing and maintenance of landscape plants), olericulture (includes production and marketing of vegetables), pomology (includes production and marketing of fruits), and post-harvest physiology which involves maintaining quality and preventing spoilage of horticultural crops.

A horticulturist, whether a gardener or a qualified graduate, has enormous responsibilities. He has to take care of plants, maintaining grass for various purposes, all aspects of wine and winemaking, maintaining the quality of and preventing the spoilage of plants and animals besides maintaining landscape plants.

Horticulture has tremendous scope in India and horticulturists are much in demand. A graduate in horticulture science can be easily absorbed in various government agencies. It is a creative work and demands patience and love for nature. One can also start a business as a floriculturist and pomologist.

Essential Qualifications: 10+2 in any stream from a recognized board

Undergraduate courses:

- B.Sc.
- B.S.

Scope in Horticulture Science:

- Government departments
- Educational institutions
- Tissue culture specialists
- Crop inspectors
- Crop production advisers
- Cropping systems engineers
- Plant breeders
- Research scientists

- Wholesale or retail business managers
- School and college teachers

Institutions for Horticulture Science: See section on agriculture on page 79.

Placements:

- State horticulture departments, National Horticulture Board (NHB), Indian Council of Agriculture Research
- Ministry of Agriculture
- Ministry of Urban Planning
- National Research Centre for Agroforestry
- National Centre for Agriculture, Economics & Policy Research

(5) Food Technology

Food Technology mainly deals with manufacturing and preservations of food products through scientific methods. Modern techniques are applied not only for processing and preservation, but for packaging and storing the basic food products like rice and wheat, oil, cereals, sugar and pulses. Besides, all the edible products which you see in the departmental stores like biscuits, pasta, breads, cakes, pastries, corn flakes and other nutritional crunches are processed in a scientific way so as to retain the chemical and microbiological properties of the products.

Due to present day lifestyle of people, especially present day youngsters, food industry is rapidly growing in India, thereby creating many employment opportunities for graduates in India. Since food is essential for life, the scope of food industry is enormous. The degree-holders are easily absorbed in food processing industries which are in abundance in India besides manufacturing industries and distilleries, research laboratories, quality control, food packaging, soft drink factories, and hotels.

Essential Qualifications: 10+2 in any stream from a recognized board

Undergraduate courses:

- B. Sc. (Food Technology)
- B. Applied Science
- Bachelor of Food Science and Technology (BFST)
- B. Tech. (Food Technology)
- Diploma and Certificate Courses

Professional Institutions: Practically all the universities in India have undergraduate courses in various subjects on Food Technology. Some are mentioned below:

- Harcourt Butler Technological Institute, Nawabganj, Kanpur
- Chaudhary Devi Lal Memorial Government Engineering College, Sirsa, Haryana
- Doon Valley Institute of Engineering & Technology Karnal, Haryana
- Haldia Institute of Technologies, Kolkata G.P.O., Kolkata, West Bengal
- Laxminarayan Institute of Technology, Nagpur, Maharashtra
- Raja Balwant Singh College, Agra, Uttar Pradesh
- Periyar University, Salem, Tamil Nadu
- College of Dairy & Food Science Technology, Udaipur, Rajasthan
- School of Microbial & Food Technology, Chandigarh, Punjab

Placements: Besides government jobs in the food industry, there is ample scope in the private sector also. Some of these are mentioned below:

- Agro Tech Foods
- Amul
- Britannia
- Cadbury India Ltd.
- Dabur India Ltd.
- Gits Food Products Pvt. Ltd.
- Godrej Industries Limited
- Hindustan Lever Limited
- ITC
- Milkfood
- MTR foods limited
- Nestle India
- Parle
- PepsiCo India
- Perfetti India

(6) Poultry Farming

Poultry farming is a branch of agriculture dealing with the raising of domesticated birds for food. These birds include chickens, turkeys, ducks, guinea fowls and geese. Chicken is the most popular dish in the world, being consumed by millions of people every day. Eggs of hens are much in demand as a breakfast food. The Food and Agriculture Organization of the United Nations some years ago estimated that there were nearly sixteen billion chickens in the world, including seven hundred million in India alone. With a population of four thousand million, China leads the table.

There are two types of poultry farming: (a) Breeding farms where poultry is raised for meat; (b) Layer farms where poultry is raised for producing eggs. It is not easy to manage such a huge population of chickens only. Through scientific way of breeding such birds, poultry farming has become a big industry. Even though their population is so huge, demand exceeds the supply. Eggs are cheap and affordable, besides being highly nutritious. Chicken meat contains about two to three times as much polyunsaturated fat as most types of red meat when measured by weight. Poultry is the second most widely eaten meat in the world after pork.

The important elements connected with poultry industry are poultry technology, feed equipment, egg farming, breeders, poultry nutrition, vaccine production and animal health. Eggs maybe small, but play a very big role in revenues and employment. Right from a single poultry farm to a street vendor, poultry farming has become a very profitable industry.

Poultry farming is relatively new in India. Dr. B.V. Rao is regarded as "the Father of the Indian poultry industry". He established Venkateshwara Hatcheries Pvt. Ltd. in 1971 in Pune through his hard work, initiative and dedication. Today, it is known the world over as "Venky's".

The work profile in poultry industry consists of classification of chicken, selection of stock, poultry equipment, breeding and chick management, broiler management, hatchery management, anatomy and physiology of chicken, poultry nutrition, poultry diseases, meat technology, marketing of poultry products, etc.

Eligibility: Class X passed or equivalent with English (for 6 month certificate course in Basic Commercial Poultry Management)

Courses:

- Certificate course in Basic Commercial Poultry Management from Dr. B.V. Rao Institute of Poultry Management & Technology (24 weeks)

- Advanced course in Poultry Management from Dr. B.V. Rao Institute of Poultry Management & Technology for graduates only (48 weeks)
- Diploma and Certificate Courses from IGNOU and NIOS
- B.V.Sc (Poultry Farming)
- Certificate in Poultry Farming (CPF)
- Basic Commercial Poultry Management
- Orientation-Guidance
- Advanced Course in Poultry Management

Professional Institutions:

1. Dr. B.V. Rao Institute of Poultry Management & Technology, Pune, Maharashtra
   Web: www.venkys.com
2. Directorate of Animal Husbandry (in various states across India)
3. Department of Animal Husbandry & Veterinary Services, Odisha

Placements: Chicken retailers, manager hatchery, slaughter manager, maintenance manager.

8

Engineering-based Courses

Engineering is translating science into technology. An engineer is imaginative and creates and designs quality products based on theoretical models of science. Simplifying complex problems in technological areas is a great challenge for an engineer. The great Indian civil engineer Sir Mokshagundam Visvesvaray who earned Bharat Ratna in 1955, is a role model for aspiring engineers. Every year, 15 September is celebrated as Engineer's Day in India in his memory. Look at Mr. E. Sreedharan who changed the living style of many with his contribution to the Delhi Metro. Alfred Hitchcock, Yasser Arafat, Jimmy Carter, and Henry Ford had engineering backgrounds too.

There was a time in mid-sixties in India when engineering graduates, particularly civil engineers, were not getting proper jobs. Thereafter, there has been no dearth of jobs. Those who are good in mathematics and physics, opt to go into the engineering sector. Before early seventies there was no competition and the marks in XII class CBSE were the main criteria. Now there is cut-throat competition, particularly in IITs. There is much demand of engineers in India and engineering is going to remain the top-most preferred career in years to come.

There are great opportunities in every field of engineering. Apart from the traditional arenas of civil, mechanical, electric engineering, one can find scope in process engineering, automation, control system, material management, field engineering and many other new areas. The engineering sector is growing rapidly in India and helps getting employment opportunities for young engineering graduates.

Earlier, very few girls opted for engineering in India, but now the scenario is changing. According to a study conducted by a group of engineers in IIT Mumbai, around 22 % of women are enrolled in engineering and technology sectors. It is observed that companies with more women perform better than their counter-parts where finance and decision-making are concerned.

Lakhs of students vie for a seat in various engineering institutions but only the most able get chance. The opportunities for employment are aplenty and many of them get campus selection even before completing their engineering education. Various institutions, both government and private, offer B.E. or B.Tech. degrees. Getting admission in IITs is a matter of prestige. The courses are usually of 4-year duration. Every science has its engineering counterpart, for engineer's job is giving a practical shape to a scientific theory. An aspirant for engineering should have skill to apply scientific knowledge to design and build machines and user-friendly devices. Below are some popular branches of engineering:

- Acoustical
- Aeronautical
- Aerospace
- Agricultural
- Applied
- Automobile
- Bio-molecular
- Chemical
- Civil

- Computer
- Electrical
- Electronics & Communication
- Environmental
- Genetic
- Industrial
- Manufacturing
- Marine
- Materials
- Mechanical
- Mining
- Molecular
- Nano Technology
- Nuclear
- Petroleum
- Process
- Structural
- Textile
- Thermal
- Urban Planning

Entry to Engineering Courses

After doing +2 from a recognized board, a candidate with science background can try the following competitions:

(1) INDIAN INSTIUTE OF TECHNOLOGY JOINT ENTRANCE EXAM) (IIT-JEE): This is considered as the toughest engineering entrance examination as the selected students get entry to Indian Institutes of Technology, which is the most prestigious among all the institutes in India. Lakhs of aspirants vie for nearly ten thousand seats to get admissions in 15 IITs at present which have around 9,000 seats including ISM Dhanbad & IISER.

The examination format consists of two objective type papers, each containing math, physics and chemistry sections. The number of institutes accepting admission through JEE: 15 IITs, ISM Dhanbad, IIT-BHU.
Web: www.jee.iitd.ac.in

(2) **ALL INDIA ENGINEERING ENTRANCE EXAM (AIEEE):** Around 27000 seats for BE/ B.Tech & 950 seats for B.Arch/ B.Planning in various institutions including National Institutes of Technology, IIITs, deemed universities, technical institutions, Delhi Technological University, Delhi and other government-funded Institutions are affiliated through this examination. The examination format consists of two objective type papers, each containing math, physics and chemistry sections.

The number of institutes accepting admission through AIEEE: 5 Indian Institute of Information Technology (IIITs) and 30 National Institutes of Technology (NITs), including Delhi Technological University (DTU), PEC University, BIT Mesra, School of Planning & Architecture, SASTRA and many other deemed universities.
Web: www.aieee.nic.in

(3) **BIRLA INSTITUTE OF TECHNOLOGY & SCIENCE ADMISSION TEST (BITSAT):** Based on the prescribed syllabus of senior secondary NCERT courses, this is relatively easier than IIT-JEE. The examination is held in BITS Pilani campuses in Pilani, Goa and Hyderabad. The duration of the exam is three hours. The examination format consists of two objective multiple-choice questions type papers, each containing math, physics and chemistry sections. It has four sections and total 150 questions. Candidates need to pass XII with at least 80% marks in aggregate in PCM with a minimum of 60% marks in each (PCM).
Web: www.bitsadmission.com

(4) **VELLORE INSTITUTE OF TECHNOLOGY (VITEE):** The examination pattern is objective exam with questions in physics, maths, chemistry and biology.
Web: www.vit.ac.in

(5) **THE INDIAN INSTITUTE OF SPACE SCIENCE AND TECHNOLOGY ALL INDIA ADMISSION TEST (ISAT):** This is Asia's first Space Institute and the first in the world to offer the complete range of undergraduate, postgraduate, doctoral programmes with specific focus on space science, technology and applications. Admissions to the undergraduate programmes (B.Tech.) at IIST are made through an All India Admission Test (ISAT).The candidates must have secured at least 70% marks in aggregate in their PCM papers in the entrance exam and 70 % in class X also. The question paper is of objective type and consists of three separate sections on physics, chemistry and mathematics.
Web: www.iist.ac.in

(6) **BHARTIYA VIDYAPEETH ENGINEERING ENTRANCE EXAM (BVPEEE): Thousands of students take this prestigious examination for 700 seats.** The entrance exam will 200 objective questions from math and physics with each subject having 100 questions.
Web: www.bharatividyapeeth.edu

(7) **AMRITA ENGINEERING ENTRANCE (AEE):** Amrita Vishwa Vidyapeetham conducts its Engineering Entrance Examination every year on an all India basis for admission to the 4-year B.Tech programmes with around 1250 seats offered in the 3 campuses at Amritapuri (Kollam), Bengaluru, and Ettimadai (Coimbatore). The exam pattern consists of only one question

paper of 3 hours duration containing 120 objective type questions in mathematics, physics and chemistry.
Web: www.amrita.edu.

Well-known Professional Institutions:

1. Indian Institute of Technology (IIT) (Bhubaneswar, Bombay, Delhi, Gandhinagar, Guwahati, Hyderabad, Indore, Jodhpur, Kanpur, Kharagpur, Madras, Mandi, Patna, Roorkee, Ropar, Varanasi.)
2. Birla Institute of Technology and Sciences (BITS) (Goa, Hyderabad, Pilani)
3. Vellore Institute of Technology (VIT), Vellore, Tamil Nadu
4. National Institute of Technology (NIT) (Agartala, Allahabad, Bhopal, Kozhikode, Delhi, Durgapur, Jaipur, Imphal, Shillong, Shillong, Dimapur, Jalandhar, Jamshedpur, Kurukshetra, Nagpur, Patna, Raipur, Raurkela, Silchar, Srinagar, Surat, Warangal.)
5. Delhi College of Engineering, Delhi
6. International Institute of Information Technology (IIIT) (Allahabad, Jabalpur, Gwalior, Kanchipuram, Vadodara, Guwahati, Hyderabad.)
7. Netaji Subhash Institute of Technology (NSIT), Delhi
8. Motilal Nehru Institute of Technology (MNIT), Allahabad, Uttar Pradesh
9. College of Engineering, Pune, Maharashtra
10. R.V. College of Engineering, Bangalore, Karnataka
11. Harcourt Butler Technological Institute (HBTI), Kanpur, Uttar Pradesh
12. Thapar Institute Of Engineering & Technology, Patiala, Punjab
13. Mumbai University Inst of Chemical Tech, Mumbai, Maharashtra

14. University Inst of Engg and Tech, Chandigarh
15. P.E.S Institute of Technology, Bangalore, Karnataka
16. National Institute of Engineering (NIE), Mysore, Karnataka
17. Veermata Jijabai Technological Institute (VJTI), Mumbai, Maharashtra
18. Madras Institute of Technology, Chennai, Tamil Nadu
19. Indian School of Mines, Dhanbad, Jharkhand
20. Osmania University College of Engineering, Hyderabad, Andhra Pradesh

Note: This list is not definitive and all inclusive. Except these colleges, there are a number of private and aided colleges run all across the country that offer the above-mentioned courses.

UNIQUE COURSES

1. Fire & Safety Engineering

Eligibility: 10+2 in science stream

Undergraduate course: B. Tech.
(University of Petroleum & Energy Studies – UPES, Dehradun)

Fire and safety engineering concerns with precautionary measures to be taken and reducing the likelihood of a fire that may results in casualties and damage of properties. This also includes planned construction of a building or carrying out of structures that are already standing as well as industrial safety solutions.

Job Categories:

- Fire and Safety Engineer
- Safety officer
- Health, Safety and Environment Engineer
- Industrial Fire and Safety Engineer
- Fire and Safety Consultant

Job Profile:

- Researching the causes of fire and determining the protection methods.
- Recommending and designing fire detection materials or equipment.
- Carrying out fire safety audits, field surveys.

2. Transport Design

This interdisciplinary program deals with fundamentals of design with specific skills of a transportation system design. The course covers a broad spectrum from personal to mass transportation. It is not only limited to automobile design but to design systems which enhance mobility for human beings and commodities. Studies include the understanding and identification of the transportation needs and issues facing the country and finding creative solutions.

Eligibility criteria

10+2 or equivalent (Minimum 60 % marks)
(UPES Engineering aptitude Test)

Undergraduate courses:

Bachelor's degree in engineering/Technology/Architecture/ Design/Interior /Design/Fine Arts/Applied Arts

Top Companies hiring students:

- Maruti Suzuki India
- Mahindra & Mahindra
- Tata Motors
- TVS Motors

- Hero Motocorp
- HAL, Bajaj Auto

Professional Institute:

University of Petroleum & Energy Studies, Energy Acres, P.O. Bidholi, via Prem Nagar, Dehradun
Web: www.upes.ac.in

9

Medical-Based Courses

(1) Physician / Surgeon (MBBS)

Considered as the most well-paying job throughout the world, a person having MBBS degree is easily absorbed in public or private hospitals. Though a doctor in medical profession is highly paid and well respected, but he/she is awefully busy and most of the time is spent in the devotion to the patient. This profession is very lucrative but only those students should join it who have patience, love for humanity and devotion.

Lakhs of aspirants appear in these examinations but only few thousands are lucky to be selected. After being selected, a student has to spend four-and-a-half years to get through but he has to do one more year of internship, making the course 5.5 years. On completing MBBS, a doctor can opt for post-graduate level studies (MD / MS) through one more entrance. In the post-graduate level, students can specialize in medicine as well as surgery. Post-graduate curriculum (MD / MS) is typically of a duration of 3 years.

Minimum qualifications to appear for MBBS course is 10 + 2 with physics, chemistry and biology subjects from a recognised board. The entry in this medical field is not easy. The competition is very tough. Some competitions are held at all-India level and some at state level. A brief description is given below:

(1) **AIIMS** (All India Institute of Medical Sciences, New Delhi): It was established in 1952. There are total 50 seats for which about 80,000 students compete from all over India.

(2) **AIPMT:** CBSE conducts All India Pre-Medical/Pre Dental Entrance Examination to select candidates for 15% merit positions in medical and dental colleges all over India.

(3) **NEET / AFMC:** National Eligibility cum Entrance Test is conducted by CBSE for admission to MBBS and dental courses in each academic year. Admission to various institutes like Armed Forces Medical College (AFMC), etc., is through the merit score in NEET.

(4) **DPMT** (Delhi University Pre-Medical Test): is a national level entrance test conducted by Delhi University to select students for admission to MBBS and BDS courses offered by various medical colleges affiliated to the University of Delhi).

(5) **CMC** (Christian Medical College): Common Entrance Test for admission to 60 seats for MBBS degree in Vellore, Tamil Nadu. It is affiliated to Dr. MGR Medical University, Chennai. The exam is generally conducted in the second week of May.

(6) **JIPMER:** Jawaharlal Institute of Post-Graduate Medical Education and Research, Puducherry

(7) **COMEDK:** Consortium of Medical, Engineering and Dental Colleges of Karnataka

(8) **GUJCET** (Gujarat Common Entrance Test): is a state-level exam conducted by the Education Department, Government of Gujarat. It is open for the candidates who belong to the state of Gujarat.

(9) **PMET:** (Punjab Medical Entrance Test) is conducted in the second week of May for admission to various medical, dental, Ayurvedic and homoeopathic colleges in Punjab.

(10) **BHU-PMT:** (Benares Hindu University All India PMT), held annually for admission to undergraduate medical courses of Benares Hindu University like MBBS, BDS, BAMS and B.Pharm.

Out of 150 seats, the break-up is 84 seats in MBBS, 38 in BDS and 33 in B.Pharm.

(11) **KMC** (Kasturba Medical College, Manipal University): Admissions are done on the basis of rank in the All India Manipal University Online Entrance Test for MBBS, BDS, MD, MS, MDS, PG Diploma aspirants. MBBS, MD, MS and PG Medical.

(12) **Mahatma Gandhi Institute of Medical Sciences, Vardha:** Total available seats: 65 which may increase to 100 seats in the near future. Of the 65, 33 seats are reserved for Maharashtra students and remaining can be filled by other state students.

Eligibility: 10+2 with science subjects including biology

Undergraduate Courses: MBBS

List of other major MBBS Entrance Examinations:

- AIMS - Amrita Institute of Medical Sciences
- AIPVT - All India Pre Veterinary Test
- All India common Entrance test, Dr. DY Patil Medical College.
- AMU Medical Entrance Exam
- DUMET - Delhi University Medical/ Dental Entrance test
- DUSET - Delhi University Super-speciality Entrance Test
- MP DMAT - All India Dental & Medical Admission Test - Madhya Pradesh
- SRM Institute of Science and Technology Medical Entrance Exam

(2) Dentistry

A dentist takes care of teeth and diseases related to teeth. With time, human teeth start decaying. Since teeth are essential to chew food, it becomes important to get artificial tooth fixed inside mouth. It is called denture. New techniques are coming whereby teeth are fixed permanently.

Essential qualifications: 10+2 with science subjects including biology

Undergraduate courses:

- Bachelor of Dental Surgery (BDS)
- Bachelor of Doctor of Dental Medicine (BMD)
- Bachelor of Medical Dentistry (B.Med Dent)
- Bachelor of Dentistry (B.Dent)
- Bachelor of Dental Science (BDSc)
- Bachelor of Oral Health in Dental Science (B. OH. DSc.)
- Graduate Diploma in Dentistry

Entry into dentistry:

Like MBBS, an aspirant has to appear for competitive examinations. After completion of the 4-year course, he or she has to do 1-year internship. After becoming a dental surgeon, one can either start private practice or work under a dentist who has all the equipment necessary for dentistry. A qualified dental surgeon can also be absorbed in government hospitals. There are around 300 colleges run by the government and the private sector offering dental education. Some of these institutions are mentioned below. A dental surgeon may add to his qualification by doing 3-years specialist course in one of the following subjects: Prosthodontics; Periodontics; Oral and Maxillofacial; Surgery; Conservative Dentistry & Endodontics; Orthodontics & Dentofacial Orthopaedics; Oral Pathology & Microbiology; Community Dentistry; Pedodontics and Preventive Dentistry; Oral Medicine Diagnosis and Radiology.

Professional Institutions:

1. Maulana Azad Institute of Dental Sciences, Delhi
   Web: www.maids.ac.in
2. Manipal College of dental Sciences, Manipal, Karnataka
   Web: www.manipal.edu
3. Government Dental College, Mumbai, Maharashtra
   Web: www.gdcmumbai.org
4. Faculty of Dental Science, King George's Medial University, Lucknow, Uttar Pradesh
   Web: www.kgmu.org
5. Government Dental College, Bangalore, Karnataka
   Web: www. www.karunadu.gov.in

Other Institutions:

- Armed Forces Medical College, Pune, Maharashtra
- Christian Dental College, Ludhiana, Punjab
- Christian Medical College, Vellore, Tamil Nadu
- Coimbatore Medical College, Tamil Nadu
- College of Dental Science & Hospital, Rau, Madhya Pradesh
- Government Dental College, Rohtak, Haryana
- Hazaribag College of Dental Sciences and Hospital, Jharkhand
- Jamia Millia Islamia, Jamia Nagar, Delhi

(3) Physiotherapy

You might have observed that when a person gets injured and breaks his hand, the orthopaedic surgeon puts a plaster on the injured part. After some weeks when the plaster is removed and the broken hand is alright, the doctor recommends to do necessary exercises of the hand. Here comes the assistance of a physiotherapist who suggests the correct way of doing exercises. Physiotherapy, a branch of modern medical science, is the treatment of deformity or malfunctioning of an organ by therapeutic measures like exercises, heat, light, water, waxing, electrical shocks, etc. The primary function of physiotherapy treatment is rehabilitation which is essential for a patient to enable him to safely return to his normal life.

Physiotherapists are always in demand. Accidents can occur at any time, whether it is some sports events, a natural calamity, or just from a fall. Rehabilitation can be of any kind: physical injury, cardiac or neurological problems, obstetrics, gynaecological, paediatrics, geriatrics, or occupational therapy. Similarly, pain management is an integral part of physiotherapy.

An experienced physiotherapist is well-paid all over the world. They are in great demand in Canada and USA. This is one reason many Indians physiotherapists move to these countries.

Eligibility criteria: 10+2 or equivalent in any stream

Undergraduate Courses:

- Bachelor of Physiotherapy (4 ½ years) (10+2; 45% aggregate)
- Bachelor of Occupational Therapy (4 ½ years) (10+2; 45% aggregate)
- BPT + MPT (5 years)
- B. Sc. – Medical Physiology (3 years) (10 + 2 with PCB 50%)

Professional Institutions:

1. Pt Deen Dayal Upadhyaya Institute for the Physically Handicapped, Delhi
   Web: www.iphnewdelhi.in

2. Faculty of Applied Sciences, Manav Rachna International University, Faridabad, Haryana
   Web: www.mriu.edu.in
3. Apollo College of Physiotherapy, Chhattisgarh
   Web: www.apollocollegedurg.com
4. Indian Institute of Health Education & Research, Patna, Bihar
   Web: www.iiher.org
5. Indira Gandhi Institute of Medical Sciences, Patna, Bihar
   Web: www.igims.org

Placements: In government and private hospitals

(4) Pharmaceutical Sciences

The Pharmaceutical industries in India have always been a very bright prospect. In this field, there are three most important activities:

(1) Manufacturing of drugs
(2) Maintenance of quality control
(3) Marketing

Accordingly, the scope in pharmaceuticals includes:

(1) Manufacturing chemist: He is an expert under whose direction and supervision, the drugs are produced. An aspirant with a graduate or postgraduate degree in pharmacy or chemistry coupled with extensive training is eligible for this important post. He should also be capable of obtaining a manufacturing license to step in. It takes many years spending huge amount of money that a new drug is released in the market after being tested by the Drugs Control Authority.

(2) Quality control: Producing medicines is a sensitive issue. It is very essential that the ultimate product is effective and as

per norms. A small mistake in mixing chemicals may cost the company very dearly. Those who have a bent of mind in chemical analysis and have thorough knowledge of the subject will find the job very satisfying. There are public and private drug testing laboratories in India whose task is to check the quality of drugs. A graduate in pharmacy can also join government agencies as an analyst.

(3) Marketing: A patient, i.e. consumer has no choice of his own to consume drugs and has to depend on a doctor's prescription. The job of a salesman is to convince doctors of the effectiveness of medicines. Obviously the salesperson should have good knowledge of the product besides being active and mobile to move around the country. Usually a trained graduate in pharmacy, chemistry or biochemistry starts his career as salesperson and with experience rises to higher echelons. He should have good communication skill as well.

National Institutes:

National Institute of Pharmaceutical Education and Research (funded by the Government of India under the Ministry of Chemicals and Fertilizers) are situated in Ahmedabad, Guwahati, Hazipur, Hyderabad, Kolkata, Mohali, and Raebareli.

Eligibility criteria: 10+2 or equivalent

Undergraduate Courses:

- B. Pharm
- B.S Pharmacy + MBA
  (dual degree; 6 years)
- B.S. Pharmacy + M Pharm
  (dual degree; 6 years)

Professional Institutions:

1. KR Mangalam University, Delhi
   Web: www. krmangalam.edu.in
2. Amity University, Noida
   Web: www.amity.edu
3. Lovely Professional University, Punjab
   Web: www.lpu.in

Other Institutes:

- Delhi Institute of Pharmaceutical Sciences and Research, Delhi
- Jamia Hamdard Faculty of Pharmacy, Delhi
- Maharaja Surajmal Institute of Pharmacy, Delhi
- University of Delhi, Delhi

Placements:

- Ranbaxy Labs: Ranbaxy is the largest pharmaceutical company in India
- Cipla: Cipla is the second largest pharmaceutical company in India.
- Dr Reddys Labs
- Lupin
- Aurobindo Pharma
- Sun Pharma
- Cadila Health
- Jubilant Life
- Wockhardt

(5) Bachelor of Ayurvedic Medicine and Surgery (BAMS)

Ayurveda is the oldest system of medicine in the world. It was practiced in India centuries back and is still in use. The *Sushruta*

Samhita and the *Charaka Samhita* are the oldest text books in ayurveda which emphasise use of natural herbs to cure diseases. According to Ayurveda, diseases occur when a patient is out of harmony with three elements called *doshas*: *Vata* (air & space – "wind"), *pitta* (fire & water – "bile") and *kapha* (water & earth – "phlegm"). The ayurvedic treatment which is holistic, eliminates impurities, reduces symptoms, increases the resistance to diseases, and increases harmony in the patient's life.

A sizeable number of Indians use ayurveda only and are satisfied with results. Ayurvedic practitioners claim that diseases like arthritice, diabetes, asthma, obesity, hypertension, spondylitis, piles, skin problems, etc., can be cured using ayurvedic medicines better than the allopathic. Medical fraternity abroad also claims the benefits of ayurvedic medicines.

The curriculum in ayurveda comprises modern anatomy, physiology, pharmacology, toxicology, forensic medicine, ENT, Ophthalmology, principles of medicine, preventive and social medicine, principles of surgery, etc. Study of ayurvedic medicines is so popular that more than one hundred colleges in India offer courses in the same. With the rise in Yoga practitioners, more patients look for ayurvedic treatment in India.

The ayurvedic treatment comprises oil massages, steam therapy, exercises, meditation, yoga, and a change of diet. At times, for those diseases and ailments which have little or no cure in allopathic system, ayurvedic treatment is the alternate. In contrast to allopathic treatment, ayurveda has no side effects.

Eligibility: 10+2 with Science (physics, chemistry and biology) and English or any other equivalent qualification recognised with 50% or more marks in the aggregate of three subjects. Selection is through all-India and state-level entrance examinations. In case of private colleges, the selection is through internal examinations.

Undergraduate Courses: Bachelor of Ayurvedic Medicine and Surgery (BAMS)

Duration: 5½ years including internship

Professional Institutions:

1. Ayurved and Unani Tibbia College, University of Delhi, Delhi
   Web: www.du.ac.in
2. Chaudhary Braham Prakash Ayurvedic Charak Sansthan, Delhi
   Web: www.cbpacs.com
3. Rashtriya Ayurveda Vidyapeeth, Delhi
   Web: www.ravdelhi.nic.in

Job profile: Ayurveda doctor, lecturer, scientist, therapist, hospital and healthcare administration, clinical research, health supervisor, companies like Dabar, Vaidyanath, etc.

Placements:

- Government/ private hospitals
- Dispensaries
- Private practice
- Colleges
- Research institutes
- Ayurveda health centres
- Spas and resorts
- Pharmaceutical companies

(6) Bachelor of Unani Medicine & Surgery (BUMS)

Unan in Arabic means Greece where 'father of medicine', great Hippocrates originated this traditional system of medicine twenty five thousand years back. The base of it is Hippocrates' humoral theory according to which the health of a person depends upon the equilibrium of the four humours present inside the body: *dam* (blood), *balgham* (phlegm), *safra* (yellow bile) and *sauda* (black bile). If the balance of these humours is disturbed, the person becomes ill. The job of a *hakim* is to bring back the four humours into equilibrium so that the health of a patient is restored.

This traditional medicine was adopted by Arabs and Persians through the efforts of scholars like Rhazes (al-Razi), Avicenna (Ibn Sena), Al-Zahrawi, and Ibn Nafis and Muslims are using it till today. It came to India around 12th century AD and barring the period of British rule, it became very popular along with ayurveda. Government of India, set up the Traditional Central Research Institutes of Unani Medicine, at Hyderabad and Lucknow, eight regional research institutes at Chennai, Bhadrak, Patna, Aligarh, Mumbai, Srinagar, Kolkata and New Delhi, six clinical research units at Allahabad, Bangalore, Karimganj, Meerut, Bhopal and Burhanpur in 2001.

Eligibility: Candidates who have passed 10+2 its equivalent with physics, chemistry and biology.

Undergraduate Courses:

Bachelor of Unani Medicine & Surgery (BUMS)

Professional Institutions: The practice of Unani medicine is performed throughout India. Some of the noted institutions are:

1. Central Council for Research in Unani Medicine, Delhi
   Web: www.ccrum.net
2. Ajmal Khan Tibbia College, Aligarh Muslim University, Aligarh, Uttar Pradesh
   Web: www.amu.ac.in

3. National Institute of Unani Medicine, Bangalore, Karnataka
   Web: www.nium.in
4. Faculty of Unani Medicine, Jamia Hamdard, New Delhi
   Web: www.jamiahamdard.edu
5. Anjuman-i- Islam's Tibbia College and Hospital, Mumbai, Maharashtra
6. ZVM Unani College and Hospital, Pune, Maharashtra.

Placements:

- Government/ private hospitals
- Dispensaries
- Private practice
- Colleges
- Research institutes
- Pharmaceutical companies

(7) Nursing

Everybody is familiar with the function of a nurse. A nurse is the second mother. Who has not heard about Florence Nightingale! A nurse takes care of the patients in the hospitals so that they recover from the ailments. After the doctors finish their job, the nurses do numerous sorts of work like giving medicines in time as prescribed by doctors, vaccinating, giving emotional support, assisting mothers in childbirth and helping patients with all kinds of their needs. Nursing includes the promotion of health, prevention of illness, and the care of ill and disabled people.

Nurses are required in every field of medicine and surgery. Right from helping surgeons in anaesthesia till the patient recovers, they work day and night. Nursing is the most diverse of all healthcare professions. They work in emergency, health management of patients, critical care, midwifery and matron, neonatal, obstetrics, orthopaedics, paediatrics, military service, schools, etc.

Nursing is one of such professions where nobody is unemployed. The moment a nurse qualifies with a degree or diploma, she is absorbed immediately in hospitals and nursing homes. Nursing profession has a long history in India but in modern times, Florence Nightingale had great impact over nursing in India. She had good knowledge of Indian conditions and worked for civilians as well as for army personnels.

The Indian Nursing Council is a national regulatory body for nurses and nurse educationin India under the Government of India, Ministry of Health & Family Welfare. There are also many registered state-level nursing councils like Delhi, Karnataka, Mizoram, Maharashtra Nursing Council, etc.

Eligibility: Minimum and maximum age for admission will be 17 and 35 years. For undergraduate courses a candidate should pass 10+2 with science (PCB) and English Core/English Elective with aggregate of 45% marks from a recognized board.

Undergraduate Courses:

- Auxiliary Nurse & Midwifery (2 years)
- General Nursing & Midwifery (3½ years)
- B. Sc. (4 years)
- For specialised education, one can pursue M.Sc. and Ph.D.

Career opportunities of nursing in India:

- Ward supervisor
- Ward nurse
- Nursing superintendent
- Community health nurse

- Teaching in nursing
- Military nursing
- Nursing service abroad

Professional Institutions:

1. College of Nursing, Armed Forces Medical College (AFMC), Pune, Maharashtra
   Web: www.afmc.nic.in
2. Christian Medical College, Ludhiana, Punjab
   Web: www.cmcludhiana.in
3. College of Nursing, AIIMS, Delhi
   Web: www.aiims.edu
4. Bharati Vidyapeeth's College of Nursing, Pune, Maharashtra
   Web: www.bharatividyapeeth.edu
5. Government College of Nursing (Hyderabad, Andhra Pradesh; Delhi; Kozhikode, Kerala)

Placements:

- All the hospitals, nursing homes and clinics
- Domestic services
- Industrial companies
- Overseas jobs
- Academic institutions

10

Computer-Based Courses

(1) Computer Applications

A computer application (also known as computer software) is the outcome of computer programming which allows the users to perform numerous tasks which were rather impossible to do manually. An application differs from an operating system which runs a computer and programming tools that are created by the computer programs. Software application can be divided into two categories:

(A) Systems software which consists of programs that interact with the computer at a primary level and includes operating systems, compilers, and utilities for managing computer resources. This manages and integrates a computer's capabilities but does not directly perform tasks that benefit the user.

(B) Applications software applies the power of particular computing system software to a particular purpose and includes database programs, word processors, and spreadsheets. This is also called end-user programs.

There are different types of application software according to particular needs. The list of applications of computers is very long. Some of these are mentioned below:

- Electronic media, e.g. Web browser and Media players
- Data management, e.g. Spreadsheet and Personal database
- Documentation, e.g. Word processing, DTP, Diagramming, Email, etc.
- Finance, e.g. arithmetic software, banking software, Clearing systems, etc.
- Entertainment, e.g. Video games, PC games, Mobile games, etc.
- Education, e.g. Classroom management, Reference software etc.
- Media, e.g. Animation, Graphic art, 3D computer graphics etc.
- Product, e.g. Hardware like computer-aided designs, Software engineering like compiler software, integrated development environment, etc.
- Simulation, e.g. scientific, aeroplanes, space simulators, etc.
- Business, e.g. Budgeting, sales analysis, business workflow, etc.

The services of a graduate in computer application (BCA) are universal. There are thousands of qualified graduates and post-graduates from India who are working abroad and getting hefty pay packages. The demand exceeds the supply. In present day time it is rather impossible to work without the aid of computers whether it is banks, education, medical field, or scores of other fields.

Eligibility: 10+2 in science stream

Undergraduate course: BCA

Institutions: Practically, the courses at different levels in computer application are being taught in all leading universlties across India.

Placements:

* Private and government agencies, and educational institutions
* Wipro Technologies
* Del, HCL, IBM, Accenture, Infosys, Mahindra BHEL, Ericsson.
* Cognizant Technologies, Convergys Information Management
* Aditya Trading Solutions
* Game designing industries
* Newspapers and magazines
* TV and films
* Academics

(2) Animation & Multimedia Design

Animation deals with making inanimate objects come alive. Multimedia concerns with various media – print, audio, video – to create an interface for the users. Whether it is advertisement, entertainment or mass media, the field of animation is very lucrative. If a person has a creative mind, he can have a successful career in advertising, animation, computer games and cartoons, Computer Generated Imagery, freelancing, multimedia designing, visual effect designing and web designing. Animation is continuing to grow at a fast rate. The qualification is not as important as the aptitude in drawing and sketching coupled with an interest in computer applications. It is a creative job and requires a lot of imagination and passion for work. Apart from a course of animation, if one has a degree or diploma in Fine Arts, it adds to his capability.

There are a number of institutions in India providing professional courses in animation, gaming and multimedia that ensures a promising career in this field. These include degree and diploma courses in digital art & animation, visual effects, graphic design & web development, gaming, 2D classical & digital animation, 3D animation, interactive e-learning & application etc. to improve artistic abilities of the students

Another field of animation is 'Game Designing'. You must have seen young children busy in their i-Pad or phone viewing and playing various kinds of video games. They seem to be so absorbed that they forget everything around. Who makes these creative videos? Of course, game designers. This field of animation is now applied in films and TV as well. Game designing also includes board games, card games and cartooning. The main purpose is entertainment, fun and educational tools.

If you are creative, imaginative, have excellent visualisation skills and a flair for programming, game designing is highly paying. You must be 'all-rounder' in the sense you have to think about the possible outcome, writing script, giving direction to the cartoonist, besides being tech-savvy and programming expert.

Eligibility criteria: 10+2 or equivalent

Undergraduate Courses:

- B. Sc. - Animation & Multimedia Technology (3 years)
- Bachelor in Animation & VFX: A comprehensive 3 years program Illustration and visualisation fundamentals.
- 2D and 3D animation
- Character animation
- Creative visualisation
- Scripting
- Digital art and design
- Modelling and texturing
- Paint effects

Job profile: Visualiser, Illustrator, Graphic Designer, Flash Animator, 2D Digital Animator, 3D Animator, 3D Artist, Lighting Artist, Rigging Artist, Creative Director, Web Designer, Multimedia Programmer, Video and Film Production Artist, Games Developer, Digital Media Artist, etc.

Opportunities in animation:

- Advertising
- Animation films
- Architecture and engineering
- E-learning
- Gaming
- Instructional design
- Multimedia
- Scientific animation
- Television entertainment
- Web designing

Professional Institutions:

1. Pearl Academy, Noida
   Web: www.pearlacademy.com
2. TGC Animation & Multimedia, Delhi
   Web: www.tgcindia.com
3. Vogue Institute of Fashion Technology, Bangalore, Karnataka
   Web: www.voguefashioninstitute.com
4. Maya Academy of Advanced Cinematics, Mumbai, Maharashtra
   Web: www.maacindia.com
5. Institute of Media Studies, Bhubaneswar, Odisha
   Web: www.imsorissa.org.in

Placements:

Future Group, Game Shastra, Google India, Newspapers, Prime Focus, Rhythm and Hues, Sony, Tata Interactive Services, TV channels, Yahoo, Leo Burnett Pte. Ltd, J. Walter Thompson / Bridge Advertising Co. Ltd, M & C Saatchi, McCann-Ericson, Ogilvy & Mather Advertising, Saatchi & Saatchi, among various others.

(3) Information Technology (IT)

India missed the industrial revolution, and as a result, the overall progress of Indian economy was slow. But with the advent of Information Technology, India has become one of the fastest developing countries in this sector. India's total IT industry's share in the global market stands at 7 %; in the IT segment the share is 4 %. Indian manufacturing sector has the highest IT spending followed by automotive, chemicals and consumer products industries.

The IT industry's share of total Indian exports increased from less than 4% in 1998 to about 25% in 2012. India made a gradual progress in IT sector. At Tata Institute of Fundamental Research, the National Centre for Software Development and Computing was instituted in 1973 and it focussed on software development. The National Informatics Centre was established in 1975 followed by the Computer Maintenance Company (CMC) in 1976. During the period between 1977-1980 the country's IT companies like Tata Consultancy Services, Infosys, Cognizant, Wipro and HCL technologies became household names. It was envisaged by the Indian government during early 80s, that electronics and telecommunications were vital to India's growth and development.

The major global information technology hubs in India are: Bengaluru, also known as 'Silicon Valley of India' which is India's leading software exporter, followed by Chennai which has the largest operations centres of TCS, and Cognizant; Hyderabad, known as Cyberabad, is a also a major IT hub in India, consisting of many multinational companies like Google, Facebook, Microsoft, Amazon and Electronic Arts, etc. Likewise Mumbai, Delhi, Gurgaon and Noida have many IT companies.

Information Technology sector is the most promising sector and is creating maximum number of job opportunities for the people. It has generated many opportunities for employment to young engineers and created 230,000 jobs in India in 2012, thus providing direct employment to about 2.8 million, and indirectly employing 9 million people. Information Technology includes developing and supporting all computer software and even hardware. The highest paid jobs are those of Information Technology managers, but even the systems engineers earn a lot.

Eligibility: 10+2 in science stream

Undergraduate courses:

- Bachelor in Information Technology/Advanced Networking
- Bachelor in IT/Applied Technology
- Bachelor in Information Technology/Information Management
- Bachelor in Multimedia and Visual Communications
- Bachelor of Science in Information Technology
- Bachelor in Computer Engineering Technology
- BCA (Bachelor of Computer Applications)

Job profiles:

- Software engineers
- Software developers
- Systems engineers
- Computer programmers

- Information Technology managers
- Java developers
- Information Technology consultants
- Network systems analysts
- Data communication analysts
- Database administrators
- Web designers

Professional Institutions:

1. Garden City College (GCC), Bangalore, Karnataka
   Web: www.gardencitycollege.edu/
2. St George College of Management, Science and Nursing, Bangalore, Karnataka
3. Sikkim Manipal University (SMU), Gangtak, Sikkim
   Web: www.smv.edu.in
4. Lovely Professional University, Punjab
   Web: www.ppu.in
5. Manav Rachna University, Faridabad, Haryana
   Web: www.mriu.edu.in
6. Amity University
   Web: www.amity.edu

Placements:

There is no field where Information Technology is not in demand. There is a massive list including robotics, analysis, networking, designing, etc.

11
Professional Courses

(1) Fashion Designing

If you have an interest in fashion and glamour and have a desire to style outfits and fashion shows and want to start your own fashion styling practice then there are lot many opportunities for you. Fashion marketing is an exciting field and there are countless opportunities in the fashion industry, commercial sector, textile and clothing machine industries besides fashion shows and couture industry, retail and export market, etc. Practical-oriented skills are essential for those intending to work in the technical and theoretical areas of fashion design. The courses provide an integrated approach, combining creativity with applied technical proficiency. The would be professionals are exposed to complete understanding of contemporary fashion designs in the global fashion industry.

Fashion in India is a growing industry. With 'fashion weeks' being organised at regular intervals all over the country, and annual shows by fashion designers in the major cities of India, this field is no doubt making its mark felt. Some of the major fashion week shows are Bridal Asia; Lakme Fashion Week; Trendz Unltd Designer Exhibition, Wills Lifestyle Fashion Week; The Bride Show, Dubai; and Asian Bride Show, London. The victories of a number of Indian beauty queens in International events such as the Miss World and Miss Universe contests have also made Indian models recognized worldwide. Fashion in India covers a whole range of clothing from ornate clothes designed for wedding ceremonies to fashion lines, sportswear and casual wear.

There is ample opportunity of employment for a qualified graduate in Fashion Designing. An aspirant can become a freelance designer and a stylists fashion advisor, can launch his/her own label, and can join fashion designer export houses too.

Eligibility criteria: 10+2 or equivalent

Courses offered: B.Sc, B. Des. (3/4 years program); B.Sc.; Diploma (short duration program)

- Fashion Design
- Fashion Technology
- Fashion Marketing
- Textile Design
- Fashion Communication
- Pattern Making
- Draping
- Knitting / Embroidery
- Fashion Styling (short duration program)
- Luxury Management (short duration program)
- Lifestyle Accessories
- Apparel Manufacturing & Merchandising

Job profile:

- Style outfits in films
- Costume Designer
- Fashion Illustrator
- Providing styling services in fashion retail

- Coordinating accessories and make up along with clothes
- Fashion Advisor/Consultant
- Fashion editor

Opportunities in Fashion:

- Premium fashion, media and entertainment industries
- Independent fashion styling practice and fashion retail
- Aviation, hospitality and premier travel companies
- Celebrity management and event companies
- Premium beauty and cosmetics
- Fashion entrepreneur

Placements: Fashion houses, media, TV channels, own boutique/ studio, academics, etc.

Professional Institutions:

1. National Institute of Fashion Technology, Delhi
   Web: www.nift.ac.in
2. Vogue Institute of Fashion Technology, Bangalore, Karnataka
   Web: www.voguefashioninstitute.com
3. Pearl Academy of Fashion, Delhi
   Web: www.pearlacademy.com
4. School of Fashion Technology, Pune, Maharashtra
   Web: www.soft.ac.in
5. National Institute of design, Ahmedabad, Gujarat
   Web: www. nid.edu

Placements:

- Apparel manufacturers
- Brand marketers
- Retailers

- Textile mills
- Home furnishing companies
- Designing studios
- Media industry

(2) Interior Designing

The study of Interior Design encompasses the study of both architectural and design content with a built environment, while focussing on the human interface within a given space. The students learn space planning, creative problem solving, communication skills and knowledge of building materials, construction, computer-aided drafting and history of design. Students are taught free-hand, architectural, and computer-aided drawings, interior colour application, internal material and finishes, environmental lighting, animation, portfolios, etc., in any interior designing course.

There is a very wide scope in interior designing for those who have interest in this field. One can become Landscape designer, Interior furnisher, Product designer, Furniture designer, Freelancer & entrepreneur, Event manager, Ramp designer, Exhibition designer, Interior designers in national and international companies and firms, and can enter in the marketing field too.

Courses:

- B.Sc. (Interior Design) (3-year program)
- BID (Bachelor of Interior Design) (3-year program)
- Diploma in Interior Design

Eligibility criteria: 10+2 or equivalent (min. 60%)

Career Opportunities:

- CAD Designer

- Commercial Interior Designer
- Design Consultant
- Exhibition Designer
- Furniture Designer
- Institutional Interior Designer
- Lighting Designer
- Residential Interior Designer
- Design Educator

Professional Institutions:

1. Indian Institute of Technology, Mumbai, Maharashtra
   Web: www.iitb.ac.in
2. National Institute of design, Ahmedabad, Gujarat
   Web: www.nid.edu
3. Sai School of Interior Design, Delhi
   Web: www.saischoolofdesign.com
4. Arch Academy of Design, Jaipur, Rajasthan
   Web: www.archedu.org
5. Sir JJ School of Applied Arts, Mumbai, Maharashtra
   Web: www.jjiaa.org

Placements: Advertisement agencies, fashion labels, departmental stores, food and beverages, hotels and publishing houses.

(3) Graphic Designing

Graphic design is the study of visual communication ideas through printed and digital presentations. The study of Graphic Design involves an in-depth understanding of a graphic designer's role in history and society. The students get opportunities to explore issues of culture, economics, and social implications of graphic design solutions. They achieve their multi-disciplinary skills to offer creative and practical solutions preparing themselves for challenging careers combining creativity, concepts and computer software skills in highly competitive advertising and publishing industries. A student opting for graphic design should have natural creativity and critical thinking. The course consists of various types of designs like icon, packaging, portfolios, logos, advertisement, brochures, catalogues, magazines, image manipulating techniques, etc.

Eligibility criteria: 10+2 or equivalent

Undergraduate Course: Bachelor of Graphic Design (3 years)

Career Opportunities:

- CAD Designer
- Commercial

Professional Institutions:

1. TGC Animation and Multimedia, Delhi
   Web: www.tgcindis.com
2. Raffles Millennium International, Delhi
   Web: www.raffles-millenium-delhi.com
3. Lovely Professional University, Punjab
   Web: www.lpu.in

Placements: Newspapers, cyber media, publication houses, fashion designing houses, design studios.

(4) Product Designing

The study of product design involves the hands-on approach to technological manufacturing skills and design management. The students learn numerous varieties of products design like lighting, furniture, electrical products, transportation and spatial design.

They also learn computer-aided design, 3D manipulation, colour analysis in 3D design, digital imaging, solid modelling, etc.

Eligibility criteria: 10+2 or equivalent

Courses offered: Bachelor of Product Design (3-year course)

Career opportunities: Product designer, toy designer, model maker, glass designer, furniture designer.

Professional Institutes:

1. Amity University, Noida
   Web: www.amity.edu
2. Raffles Millennium International, Delhi
   Web: www.raffles-millenium-delhi.com
3. Sushant School of Design, Delhi
   Web: www.ansaluniversity.edu.in
4. GD Goenka University, Haryana
   Web: www.goenkaglobal.com
5. Lovely Professional University, Punjab
   Web: www.lpu.in

(5) Jewellery Designing & Gemology

Students learn to explore a variety of areas within traditional and contemporary jewellery designs which emphasise on creativity, innovation, experimentation, and the material application of technical skills. The course includes cultural studies, drawing skills, colour analysis in 3D design, 3D manipulation, digital imaging, computer-aided design, metalwork, enamelling and glass, silver-smithing, gold, stone setting, etc.

India probably has the biggest gem industry in the world and also is the largest consumer of gold. India is already the largest diamond cutting and polishing centre in the world. The Indian jewellery and gems market is one of the fastest growing industries in the world.

Eligibility criteria: 10+2 or equivalent

Undergraduate Course:

* B. Sc. (Jewellery Design)
* Diploma in Jewellery Design
* Diploma in Gemology (1-year course)

Professional Institutes:

1. Aarshi Management Solutions (AMS) (For women only), Delhi
   Web: aarshimanagementsolutions.com
2. GD Goenka University, Haryana
   Web: www.goenkaglobal.co
3. New Delhi YMCA, Delhi
   Web: www.newdelhiymca.org
4. IMS-Design & Innovation Academy, Noida
   Web: www.diaindia.co.in

Placements: Jewellery brands, fashion studios, film industry, brands making accessories.

(6) Textile Designing

You come across various types of patterns of shirts, saris and other clothing when you go to the market. At times you wonder the varieties of pattern of saris and find that no two products are similar. Textile designing is an art as well as a science. It involves your imagination and creativity as well as your aesthetic sense. It is a process from the raw material into finished product and deals with creating designs for various types of fabrics and yarns like knitted, woven, non-woven and designing patterns for clothes, towels, carpets, and household textile. It is the core of the fashion world.

An undergraduate in textile designing learns many skills while doing the course, such as drawing and sketching, textile fibres, colour, composition and basic textile design for printing and weaving. The programme includes dyeing techniques, printing methods, sewing techniques, construction of fabrics and surface design, and various mediums of surface design, like prints, woven, dyed and embroidered. At present, many professional textile designers employ computer-aided design software for this purpose. It involves an understanding of traditional techniques as well as modern mass production methods.

There is a lot of scope for graduates in textile designing sectors like export houses, buying houses, craft sector, apparel and global brands, entrepreneur, etc. Textile industry is the second largest employer after the agricultural sector and contributes 4 % to the country's GDP and 13.5 % to the annual export earnings. A textile designer can be employed in the garment, fashion, home furnishing and the interiors segment among other industries.

Eligibility criteria: 10+2 or equivalent

Undergraduate Course:

- B. Des. (Textile Design)
- B. Des. (Knitwear Design)
- B. Des. (Leather Design)
- B. Des. (Accessory Design)
- B. Des. (Fashion Communication)
- B. F. Tech. (Apparel Production)

Professional Institutions:

1. National Institute of Fashion Technology, Delhi (with branches in Bangalore, Bhopal, Chennai, Gandhinagar, Hyderabad, Kangra, Kannur, Kolkata, Mumbai
   Web: www.nift.ac.in
2. National Institute of Design, Ahmedabad, Gujarat
   Web: www.nid.edu
3. Pearl Academy of Fashion, Delhi
   Web: www.pearlacademy.com
4. School of Fashion Technology, Pune, Maharashtra
   Web: www.softpune.com

Placements: Apparel houses, export agencies, merchandising units, design studios, clothing companies, mills, boutiques, furnishing houses, etc.

12

Armed Forces

Joining Indian Armed Forces means a set career of honour, discipline and patriotism. The life in armed forces is totally different from civilian lives. It is not only prestigious but adventurous as well. There is no other career where one learns so many things during one's training and afterwards. Think of a cadet who becomes an officer at a tender age and with time advances to higher echelon. People in armed forces not only get respect from all walks of life but appreciation too, because they are the defenders of country's borders. It is not only during war time that they are required, but also in peace time during natural calamities.

One great advantage in joining armed forces is moving from place to place across the country, living an exclusive life. Even after retirement, there is no dearth of employment for them in getting decent jobs.

Entrance into Armed Forces:

The armed forces broadly comprise Army, Air Force and Navy. For all these wings an examination is conducted through Union Public Service Commission (UPSC) for permanent commission in the armed forces. The examination is conducted twice a year – in the month of April and in December. You must have cleared

10 +2 with science subjects with a minimum score of 70% in physics, chemistry and mathematics (you can also appear in the examinations if you are studying in Class XII) provided you are in the age group 16½ and 19 and are unmarried. After clearing all the examinations – written test, interview and medical test – you are qualified to join the National Defence Academy (NDA) based in Kharakwasla, Pune. It goes for three years and one also earns a Bachelor's Degree by Jawaharlal Nehru University, New Delhi. The fourth year of the exclusive training is any of the three wings – Army, Air Force and Navy.

The examination pattern is as follows:

(1) **Written Examination:** The NDA written examination consists of two papers:

(a) Mathematics: The course covered is that of +2 level. (300 marks)

(b) General Ability Test: This too is divided in to (i) English (200 marks) and (ii) General Knowledge (400 marks)

Both are objective type of tests having multiple choice questions. Each question carries four marks. The time duration is 2½ hours (150 minutes). There is penalty for wrong answers.

Those candidates who are qualified for interview are to face a tough session with Service Selection Board (SSB)

(2) **Interview:** In order to select right candidates, the SSB grills the aspirant for 5 days, asking various questions to judge their potentialities – intelligence and personality. Once getting through, the candidates have one more barrier – medical fitness.

(3) **Medical Test:** The Services Medical Board conducts all sort of medical examinations. If medically fit, the candidates join the National Defence Academy.

After getting training at NDA, those who preferred Army go to one year further training at the Indian Military Academy (IMA) at Dehradun; the cadets for Air Force take further training at the Air Force Academy at Dindigul (Secundrabad); and for Navy the training centre is the Indian Naval Academy at Ezhimala or the Officers' Training Academy, Chennai.

Written Examination Centres: Agartala, Ahmedabad, Bangalore, Bareilly, Bhopal, Chandigarh, Chennai, Cuttack, Dehradun, Dharwad, Dispur, Gangtok, Hyderabad, Imphal, Itanagar, Jaipur, Jammu, Jorhat, Kochi, Kohima, Kolkata, Lucknow, Madurai, Mumbai, Nagpur, Panaji, Patna, Raipur, Ranchi, Sambalpur, Shillong, Shimla, Srinagar, Tirupati, Udaipur, and Visakhapatnam.

Other than NDA, entry to the three armed forces is open for graduates. These include Indian Military Academy (IMA) at Dehradun, College of Military Engineering (CME) at Pune, the Officers' training Academy, Chennai for Short Service Commission. After being recruited in the Indian Armed Forces, officers get chance for specialised courses in a number of defence institutions which help them to top ranks.

13

Studying Abroad

Due to rising Indian economy and globalisation, now many Indian students are studying abroad. It is a privilege to have a foreign degree. Though only rich people can afford to study abroad, the ordinary middle class students can get scholarships to study in developing countries like the UK, the USA, Canada, Germany, Italy, New Zealand, Australia and South Africa. The popular fields of study are as follows.

- **Management**
  MBA, Banking, Finance, Marketing, Accounting, HR, Supply Chain, Sports.
- **Engineering**
  BE, MTech, Civil, Telecom, Energy & Planning, Mechanical, Biotechnology, Nanotechnology, Medical, Marine.
- **Design**
  Interior Design, Architecture, Fashion & Textile Design, Animation.
- **Information Technology**
  BCA, MCA, BIT, MIT, Networking, ERP, Security, Software.
- **Hospitality, Tourism & Aviation**
  Hotel Management, Cookery, Patisserie & Bakery, Events, Entertainment, Resort Management, Travel

- **Other popular courses**
  Law, Nursing, Pharmacy, Health Management, Education, Journalism & communication.

A. **Germany**

Once Angela Merkel, Chancellor and Head of the German government remarked, "We are proud to welcome more than 5,000 Indian students in Germany so far." Every year, many Indian students opt for business and management education in Germany.

According to Leopard-Theodor Heldman, the Consul General of the Federal Republic of Germany in Mumbai, "For me an objective worth pursuing is that in the future many more Indian students acquire Doctorate, Master's or Bachelor's degrees in Germany.

Germany has around 350 state-funded universities catering to almost every subject. There is one consultancy by the name *The Calculus* which has arrangement with a number of universities for various science-based programmes. It is the largest German education consultancy in India which helps students in obtaining visa and admissions.

Undergraduate Course: B.Sc, B.Tech, BBA, MBA.

Eligibility: 10+2 (PCM / PCB)

The Calculus
Web: www.thecalculusgroup.com

B. **CBS, Germany**

One of the most famous institutions in Germany as well as one of the world's best business schools is the Cologne Business School (CBS). It is the oldest network of private schools and universities in Germany. It was established in 1908 and is maintaining its standard and reputation. Through the close contact with the private sectors, CBS has been able to provide great career prospects for graduates.

Chitkara University in Chandigarh is a partner university with Cologne Business School.

Undergraduate Course:

- Bachelor of Arts in International Business
- Bachelor of Arts in International Culture and Management
- Bachelor of Arts in International Media Management
- Bachelor of Arts in General Management

Besides the above information, Cologne Business School offers an own scholarship programme depending on the financial status of a student.

Duration of courses: 3 years

Placements: Scores of world-class companies spread over Europe, USA, Asia, Australia, i.e. Apple Inc., Daimler AG, Google Inc., Foursquare, IBM, Deutschland, Lufthansa, Siemens AG, Vodafone, etc., offer jobs to these professionals.
Web: www.cbs-edy.de

C. **Italy / US / New Zealand**

The Laureate International Universities network based in Italy, *Neovo Accademia di Belle Art* (NABA), Milano, Italy conducts courses in Media Design, Architecture and Art in various countries: Media Design School in Santa Fe University of Art and Design, and New School of Architecture and Design.

Milan: Milan is said to be the world capital of fashion and design and has inspired artists and designers for centuries. The *Nuova Accademia Di Belle Arti Milano* is an outstanding school of arts and design. It caters the need of around 1800 students from over 50 countries from the expertise of 300 professionals.

Courses: Bachelor of Arts Degree Programmes

- Painting and Visual Arts
- Design
- Fashion Design
- Graphic Design and Art Direction
- Media Design and Multimedia Arts
- Theatre and Exhibit Design

D. **Santa Fe, New Mexico, USA**

Santa Fe in New Mexico, USA is considered an artistic and cultural haven and is the home to thousands of artists. This beautiful city has around 250 galleries and organizes cultural festivals from time to time.

Undergraduate Course:

(1) **Bachelor of Arts Degree Programmes**

- Contemporary Music
- Creative Writing and Literature
- Moving Image Arts (Film/Video)
- Photography
- Studio Arts
- Theatre Design
- Theatre Performances

(2) **Bachelor of Fine Arts Degree Programmes**

- Digital Arts

- Graphic Design
- Photography
- Studio Arts
- Theatre with specializations in Acting, Music Theatre, Design/Technical, and Dance.

(3) Bachelor of Business Administration

- Arts Management

Eligibility: 10+2 or equivalent

E. San Diego, California, USA

New School of Architecture and Design in California is one of the finest architecture schools in the United States which provides a beautiful laboratory for experimentation and exploration of urban conditions.

New School of Architecture and Design.

Undergraduate Course:

- Bachelor of Architecture
- Bachelor of Arts in Architecture
- Bachelor of Landscape Architecture
- Bachelor of Science in Construction Management
- Bachelor of Science in Digital Media Arts

F. Auckland, New Zealand

This city in New Zealand is well known for all aspects of digital media designs that include visual effects, 3D animation, interactive gaming and advertisements. It gives an opportunity to learn creative ideas to make your career joyful.

Media Design School, Auckland, New Zealand.

Undergraduate Course:

- Bachelor of Art and Design
- Bachelor of Software Engineering
- Bachelor of Creative Technologies

This institute also provides Diploma Programmes as follows:

- 3D Computer Animation
- Creative Advertising
- Digital Media
- Graphic Design
- Interactive Gaming
- Visual Effects and Motion Graphics

Eligibility: 10+2 or equivalent

Placements: Versace, Swatch, The Disney Channel, Paramount Pictures, HBO, McCanne Worldgroup, Los Angeles Opera, Audi, MTV, Nike, Canon, Volkswagen, Pepsi and many more.

G. **Switzerland**

Schweizerische Textilfachschule (STF) (Swiss Textile College, STC) based in Waittwil, Switzerland is a top class institution which offers a Bachelor (Hons.) in Textile Technology & Design degree with practical tutorial. STF deploys innovative software systems, not only in the CAD of clothing and textiles but also in the creation of alternative fashions. Studying at the STF is not just learning to sew and print, it is also learning how to use the appropriate technology for each specific case. Such technologies include ultrasonic welding systems, body scanning, virtual prototyping (3D), plasma technology and various types of coatings

Undergraduate Course:

(1) **Bachelor (Hons) in Textile Technology & Design**

The area of design and technology includes a wild field of activity ranging from design, product development process and technology development to production management, quality performance and consultancy.

(2) **Bachelor (Hons) in Fashion Design & Textile Technology (Design Major)**

The students are provided with in-depth training in the techniques of fashion design.

Eligibility: (for 1) Higher education entrance qualification (A-Level) or Vocational college qualification (A-Level); (for 2) Vocational qualification or equivalent qualification from secondary school or A-Level.

Course duration: 3 years
Web: www.swisstextilecollege.ch

H. **Canada**

There are some excellent universities in Canada where Indian students can pursue education for which there is an Application Centres in Delhi and Gurgaon which gives reliable and authentic information on education in Canadian universities like St. Mary's University, The University of Winnipeg, University of Victoria, Thomas University, and Sault College. At the end of the programme, a student is eligible for work permits.

More information can be obtained from www.canada123.org

Undergraduate Programmes:

- Engineering
- Information Technology
- Nanoscience
- Biotechnology
- Business
- Hotel Management
- Aviation
- Health
- Media Studies
- Psychology
- Film

Top colleges in Canada:

- University of Waterloo
- University of British Columbia
- University of Manitoba
- University of Alberta
- Universite de Montreal
- University of Victoria

I. Malaysia

The Asia Pacific University of Technology and Innovation (APU) based in Kuala Lumpur , Malaysia, is an outstanding institution of higher studies which is in partnership with Staffordshire University in United Kingdom and is in collaboration with a number of universities in Australia, Canada, New Zealand and Netherlands. This institution has bagged numerous international awards. The students after passing their graduation are much sought after by employers the world over.

The APU in association with Staffordshire University has a

number of programmes for students after doing their 10+2 or equivalent courses:

(1) School of Computing & Technology:

- B. Sc. (Hons.) in Information Technology
- B. Sc. (Hons.) in Software Engineering
- B. Sc. (Hons.) in Internet Technology
- B. Sc. (Hons.) Entreprise Computing
- B. Sc. (Hons.) Technopreneurship
- B. Sc. (Hons.) in Multimedia Technology
- B. Sc. (Hons.) Web Media Technology
- B. Sc. (Hons.) in Media Informatics

(2) School of Engineering:

* BEng(Hons.) in Electrical & Electronics Engineering
* BEng(Hons.) in Telecommunication Engineering
* BEng(Hons.) in Mechatronic Engineering

(3) School of Accounting Finance & Quantitative Studies

* B. A. (Hons.) in Accounting and Finance
* Bachelor in Banking and Finance (Hons.)
* B. Sc. (Hons.) in Actuarial Studies)
* B. Sc. (Hons.) in Management Science

(4) School of Business & Management

* B. A. (Hons.) in Business Management
* B. A. (Hons.) in International Business Management
* B. A. (Hons.) in Marketing Management
* B. A. (Hons.) in Human Resource Management
* B. A. (Hons.) in Tourism Management
* B. A. (Hons.) in Services Management

* B. A. (Hons.) in Media Marketing
* B. Sc. (Hons.) in Media Informatics

Address:

Asia Pacific University of Technology and Innovation,
Web: www.apu.edu.my

New Delhi Office:
A-37, Naraina Industrial Office, Phase II,
New Delhi-110 028
Web: www.studymalaysia.asia

Note: There are unlimited destinations for Indian students for pursuing higher studies. There are many private agencies who provide necessary help for admissions throughout the world.

RECOMMENDED READING

ISBN : 9789382891109
Size : 7.75" x 5.1"
Extent : 264
Binding : PB
Subject : Reference

The New Students' Companion

A treasure house of knowledge

Meenakshi

Thomas Huxley sums up the message of learning as follows:

"Try to learn something about everything and everything about something."

The New Students' Companion comprises information on Indian history, politics, geography of India and the world, universe and space, economy, science and technology, sports, culture, mathematics, and many more.

Get set to dive into invaluable information with this mandatory addition to your book shelf.

Meenakshi is working as an Associate Professor and strives to enhance learning skills.

ISBN : 9789382891062
Size : 7.75" x 5.1"
Extent : 208
Binding : PB
Subject : Reference

What They Don't Teach at School

The Joy of Knowledge

Vijaya Khandurie

Do you know the name of the 13th century ruler in the Indian subcontinent who died while playing Polo?

Have you seen an animal that can clean its own ears with its tongue?

Get set for more such facts from varied fields of History, Politics, Economy, Religion, Culture, Literature, Environment, Science, Sports, Astronomy and many others, all in one book.

Vijaya Khandurie has put together interesting facts, thanks to his 45 years in education.